Selling Yourself
into the
Right Job

Selling Yourself into the Right Job

The Marketing Edge

by Stuart Herst

Designed by Karen A. Yops

Library of Congress Cataloging in Publication Data
Herst, Stuart, 1918–
   Selling yourself into the right job: the marketing edge.

   1. Applications for positions. I. Title.
HF5383.H47   650.1′4   80–13341
ISBN 0-695-81442-7

First Printing

Contents

Psychological Test. How to Cheat a Little. Don't Show Any
Impatience. Sentence-Completion Tests. Draw-a-Picture Tests.
Thematic Apperception Tests. Self-Description Words.

Introduction

The odds are you will *sell* yourself into your next job rather than be hired because you are the most qualified candidate available for the position. In fact, unless you were employed by a friend or relative, you *sold* yourself into your present or last position. Of course, what you sold and will sell is the fact or the impression that you are the most qualified candidate. You also sell your potential and your personality as the type of person your new boss wants to have on the company team.

This book will give you a commonsense step-by-step approach to selling yourself into a better job. It comes from a long career—almost fifteen years—of successfully teaching executives how to set career goals and attain them. As a principal with a firm engaged both in personal marketing consulting and in outplacement consulting for displaced corporate executives, I have firsthand experience plus knowledge gained from working with clients and studying the results.

I have thought out many of these ideas merely by sitting down and considering them from the viewpoint of the prospective employer as well as that of the job searcher.

Personnel people won't like this book. I probably worked more with them before becoming a consultant than in the fifteen years since. I have put much time and thought into how to get around them and reach the *real* decision makers when it comes to hiring managers and executives. You will read about clients who have been hired by a company after the company's own personnel department had turned them down. That is not an unusual occurrence.

Psychologists won't like this book, as it teaches you how to give favorable impressions about yourself on their tests.

Many consultants and placement and employment agency people will dislike this book, since it pulls no punches in telling you why and how some of them are bad and how to choose the good ones to use if you can personally benefit from their services.

You will like this book because it is written for you—to help you. It contains methods and ideas never before published. Probably more important, it teaches you why and how to hold back information to present yourself in the best light or preserve your bargaining stance. For example, employment agencies and personnel types want you to put your salary history on your resume. Do that and, unlike many of our clients, you won't get the next job at 30 to 50 percent more than your present salary. In fact, we teach our clients—as does this book— how *not* to use resumes because they are primarily used to cut down the list of applicants to be interviewed.

Chapters 1 and 2 introduce you to the job-search campaign, telling you what to expect and how to set career goals for yourself. The rest of the book is the real meat, since it shows you how to proceed and why certain methods are good and others bad.

Finally, in the knowledge that these methods will work for you, the last chapter tells you how to start paving the way for raises and promotions, or even another job with your new company or a different one, the very day you start with your new employer.

Selling Yourself
into the
Right Job

1

The Phases of Your Job-Search Campaign

You should mentally divide your job-search campaign into seven phases. I said mentally because actually some phases must overlap. For instance, you should always seek additional interviews—even after you truly expect an offer from a particular company. Even after making an offer or indicating an offer will come, companies have been known to change their minds, promote somebody from within, decide not to add a new person, or find a candidate who has a better background for their particular needs. Sometimes they even come up with a lower salary than the one originally discussed. So, keep pushing for more interviews until you have a firm offer and have accepted it.

First: **Learning the Product—What *You* Will Sell**

The first phase is obviously learning the product: You are the product to be sold by mail, by phone, and, ultimately, in person. You have to decide on the type of position to seek. You must pick out your selling points and decide how to best present them to a prospective employer. This will be interesting but exacting work. However, you will find it satisfying. Learning the product is the theme of the next chapter in this book.

13

Second: **Creating *Your* Sales Tools**

Phase two gets down to the business of creating sales tools to make your prospects want to interview you. This is the time and place to tell you how people get their new jobs. Below the executive level, employment agencies and ad answers *probably* do best. Why probably? It depends on whom you listen to. I have seen or heard of many surveys on how new jobs were found. The difference in the figures, I think, is often due to the particular desires of either the maker of the surveys or the firm planning to use the results to further its own sales or ideas.

One survey of 1,000 individuals described as executives by the survey user reported that 30 percent were successful through answering ads and 27 percent via the employment agency route. Over the years, I've guided several hundred executives to better jobs. I label an executive as a person in a management position (senior, middle, or lower) who earns more than $20,000. My clients average just more than $40,000 in annual base pay. At any rate, a majority of the people I've worked with embarked on their new career as a result of a carefully worded, individually typed sales letter sent to an equally carefully selected mailing list.

The survey of 1,000 reported that 6 percent of the respondents found their present position by the mailing of a sales letter. However, only 15 percent used the sales-letter approach. You don't need your calculator to find the sales letter was successful for 40 percent of those who used it. It worked for more than 50 percent of my clients. The how-to of sales letters will be discussed at length in chapter 4, complete with examples of actual letters and their results.

I've seen letters to one company resulting in jobs with another company. It's not unusual to get a call (and a job) from a company that you wrote to months or even years ago. You might then graduate from the job acquired through the original mailing to a better position. John B. did that after more than two happy years with the first firm.

As you would expect, a selling resume is another sales tool. But, beware of resumes. They are primarily used by the prospective employer as an easy way to weed out excess candidates for a position. You will learn how to prepare and use resumes in chapter 5, which is devoted exclusively to this most misunderstood and abused job-search tool.

Answering ads, mentioned above, is an art rather than a science. There are several reasons why the job hunter should answer ads. Whether or not it results in a job offer, answering ads correctly will certainly help prepare you to handle yourself well in interviews. Every ad you answer teaches you how to sell yourself. It is one of the most important things I can teach any job hunter. Consider each ad you answer as a practice interview in writing.

Other sales tools you should use include a combination sales and thank-you letter to go out as soon as possible after each interview, letters to references and personal contacts, an interview kit carefully used to overcome possible credibility gaps, and letters to people who reply to your sales letter in the negative. All these will be discussed at their proper time.

Third: Preparing Yourself for Interviews

The third phase in your job-search campaign is preparing yourself for the interviews these sales tools will surely get you. You have learned about yourself and what you as a particular individual have to sell when selling yourself. You are not going to bore your prospective employer with facts not related to your ability to fill his or her needs. But you *are* going to do research on the company to have a good idea as to its needs. So, phase three begins as you learn about yourself in phase one. It continues in the future as you prepare yourself for each interview. Later in this book we shall examine how you should prepare for individual interviews.

Fourth: Getting Interviews

The important fourth phase is getting interviews. In using the psychological approach necessary, be sure to recognize that you are the low man on the totem pole at this point. Somebody out there has the power to give you the job you want, and you must learn the proper approaches that will earn you consideration as a likely candidate *to fill his or her needs.*

This means you should go all out to contact prospective employers when they can be expected to be in a good mood and more receptive to your candidacy. Always try to put yourself in their shoes. Consider in advance how they might react to your actions. For example, don't send the sales letter to arrive on a Monday. I even suggest you go so far as to avoid Monday interviews. Normally, Mondays are the busiest day of the week for executives. They might be too busy or harassed to give you the attention you deserve. How do you avoid a Monday interview if it is suggested? Simple. Just say you have another interview scheduled then. Suggest Tuesday. You will gain more respect if you imply that others are interested in hiring you.

Many interviews will be arranged through telephone calls. You would be wise not to phone a busy executive on a Monday. He or she may be too busy to give you the time you want for that phone conversation. Also, avoid phoning on Friday afternoons. Some executives have their minds on the golf course or the coming weekend. On the other hand, if your prospective employer suggests an interview any time on a Friday, Saturday, or even Sunday, you will probably have a good session. The odds are that you will get undivided attention.

Fifth: Selling Yourself in Interviews

Our fifth phase is most important. It concerns *selling yourself* in interviews. This is where the chips are down. Interviewing techniques deserve a full chapter by themselves. (See chapter 15.) However, you will learn much about selling yourself as you read my ideas on how best to answer ads, write sales letters and resumes, use resumes, etc. By now you should realize that every paragraph in this book is designed to help make you a better salesperson of your most important product: your own unique abilities.

Sixth: Negotiating *Your* Salary and Perquisites

Phase six in your job-search campaign involves negotiating salary and, possibly, fringe benefits. Like the shoemaker's children who go without shoes, most job seekers can properly represent their company but don't do well for themselves as negotiators. You'll learn the methodology later in proper sequence.

Seventh: Evaluating (and Possibly Renegotiating) Your Offers

If properly followed, this, the final, phase will result in your accepting the *right job* at the *right price.* I call this evaluating (and possibly renegotiating) offers. Obviously, you want to rate each offer with respect to how it fits your personal career plan. Is it the right type of company for you? Will it provide the autonomy (or supervision) you need to function happily? Can you respect and work well with your new boss? You must make an overall decision as to whether or not you want to be part of the company.

Renegotiation is a matter that doesn't always come up with a company that earns yes answers to all the above. If you believe you are entitled to more dollars or fringes, a better title, or possibly a different spot in the organization, you should look for an opening or a way to do some renegotiating. This is the time you should discuss both the interview and the offer with a consultant or a friend who holds a true executive-level position. He or she may see a valid point of renegotiation that you couldn't perceive only because you are too close to the situation. You are emotionally involved, but your adviser is detached.

Helping clients renegotiate is one of my biggest thrills. Sometimes it isn't money that we negotiate. Edward B. and I spent a few hours going over an offer he was expecting. We knew he would receive an offer in the next day's interview because it was to be his seventh session, and, furthermore, he had been told the "necessaries" were going to be discussed. We knew base pay and bonus would be just about $60,000. Ed wanted the new company to pay the broker's commission and the lawyer's fees on the sale of his home. He also wanted the company to provide him with a Buick, as one came with his then present job.

I taught Ed how to hold out for a $60,000 base or a base and guaranteed bonus in that amount or more. His current salary was in the mid-forties. Although Ed agreed with me that he would make a big profit on the sale of his home, he was adamant regarding reimbursement of his selling expenses. I insisted that he not bring the matter up till salary had been set. Rule: Never talk fringes till salary has at least been discussed. I did get Ed to agree not to talk about a Buick or any particular car. He agreed to accept a car similar to those driven by others at his level.

The next day a happy client phoned me. The company had offered a base pay under $60,000 but had come up without hesitation when Ed merely asked for more! In fact, he had been told he would earn a bonus of 40 percent his first year. Ed had then made the decision to listen to his consultant and not bring up the expenses of selling his home. After all, the $24,000 bonus plus a 33 percent raise would more than cover those costs.

Ed was also wise in not bringing up the matter of the Buick. Three days after he had started the job, he phoned me to report that he had been asked what kind of car he wanted—a Cadillac or a Lincoln!

As I said, money is not always the most important element in renegotiating. Tom C., a Management Information Systems manager, received an offer exactly $500 less than he and I felt the job should pay. In discussing what took place in the interview, I could see that Tom's prospective boss had offered him $500 less to feel tight control over him. Since Tom had already accepted the offer, I told him what to say (the words are pertinent to only that particular situation) in asking for $500 more. When he did, the boss embraced Tom and said, "I'm proud you're working for me." The $500 was not the element here. Tom's pride and the boss's understanding were more important.

Being Flexible in Using These Phases

This chapter has given you an overview of what a job-search campaign entails. Remember, all these phases overlap and are not to be used as a step-by-step approach. Instead, whenever possible, use the various marketing tools and techniques discussed in this book in the order in which they are treated. By doing so, you will end up with many interviews and more than one job offer.

2

Realistic Career Goals

If you are to sell yourself into a new position, you must know not only what you have to sell but also the type of position you truly want—and can fill. You must become very introspective and honest with yourself. If you cannot be objective or if you feel you are not truly describing yourself, it would probably be wise to seek outside help. Go to one or, at the most, two friends whose judgment you respect, or use the professional services of an industrial psychologist or a career consultant.

Know *Your* Personality

The professionals will be able to establish many facts about you. Some may be a bit of a surprise, but others may confirm or strengthen what you already knew. At any rate, whether it be with the help of objective, perceptive friends, a professional, or just your own observations, you should actually learn several things about yourself, such as:

- *Your true motivations.* What are your needs? Which are the most important to you? Rate yourself on achievement, ego, dominance, autonomy, security, a supportive boss, and order and structure imposed by others. You might have a negative attitude or resistance to some of them. For example, many good salesmen need autonomy and abhor routine and order and structure. Figure 1 will help you not only indentify some of your motivations but also recognize some career goals.

- *Your strengths.* Rate your own intelligence honestly. How does it stack up with that of your peers or with high-level executives? Are you articulate? Are you better with the written word than the spoken one? Better with numbers than words? Are you a hard worker, responsible, conscientious? Achievement- or results-oriented? Do you get along well with your superiors, peers, and subordinates?

- *Your weaknesses.* Do you use your intelligence well? Apply common sense? Are you apolitical or nonpolitical? Impatient with people who don't meet your standards? Impulsive or compulsive? Deferential or subservient to authority? Inarticulate or too much of a talker—actually verbose? Insensitive to your impact on others to the point that you relate better to things than to people?

Figure 2 is a portion of a form my clients fill out before meeting with me or our psychologist. Filling it out now will help you answer the questions in figure 1, learn about yourself, and set career goals.

Write Up Your Job History

Put your employment history down on paper, in reverse chronological order. For each employer, list your titles, your duties, and the functions you liked plus those you disliked. Then, thinking about those jobs, indicate your accomplishments in some detail. Go beyond your employment and note accomplishments relative to your home, family, education, sports, and social and church life. What changes would you have liked to make in any of these activities?

Fig. 1 _____

On a scale of 1 (low) to 5 (high), rate your abilities and desires
as to being:

1. An accountant or statistician. Are you good with figures? Do
   you enjoy keeping or interpreting figures representing such
   things as sales, trends, inventory?   _____

2. A scientist, architect, or engineer. Do you like using applied
   skills, research, testing, or company results to get the
   right answers? Do you want to know how, what, when, why?   _____

3. A performer--the center of attraction. A salesperson, a boss,
   even a lowly clerk, must sometimes be in the limelight.   _____

4. A salesperson--a persuader who influences others. Anybody
   selling his or her own ideas or image as well as the company's
   products, services, or image is a salesperson.   _____

5. A writer or speaker--a user of words and thoughts to convey
   ideas, teach, sell, motivate, get along with others.   _____

6. Of service (help) to others. Do you enjoy making things better
   or easier for the next person on either a one-to-one or mass
   basis?   _____

7. A manager--directing others. Have you been a leader in social,
   school, association, or business activities?   _____

8. A lone worker. Do you function better if left alone to do
   things your way without too much contact with superiors, peers,
   or subordinates?   _____

9. A craftsman or a craftswoman. Do you like to build or repair
   things with your hands?   _____

10. An inventor or innovator. Are you creative? Do you enjoy
    using your imagination and skills to develop or improve new
    products, ideas, or systems?   _____

11. A success in the world of the outdoors. Would you rather
    be doing a job outside--away from a desk?   _____

12. The boss. Would you be happiest running your own business?
    With or without partners? Do you want the freedom and
    independence ascribed to bosses? Do you want to own something
    important?   _____

Which three of the above tendencies have most fashioned your
successes or achievements?   _____

                                                                _____

                                                                _____

Fig. 2

1. What do you consider your strengths (assets) as an executive?
   Which functions do you enjoy the most? _____
   _____
   _____
   _____

2. What are your weaknesses (liabilities)? Which functions
   do you dislike? _____
   _____
   _____
   _____

3. How do you get along with your superiors? What do they
   generally think of you? _____
   _____
   _____
   _____

4. As above, describe your relationships with people at your own
   level. _____
   _____
   _____
   _____

5. As above, describe relationships with your subordinates. _____
   _____
   _____
   _____
   _____

6. Are you qualified to be chief executive officer of a company? _____

   If yes, how big a company? _____

7. What various positions can you hold based on your education,
   experience, personality, and interest? _____

   _____

   _____

   _____

   _____

8. Forgetting qualifications, what would you <u>really</u> enjoy as an
   occupation? Please list as many functions as occur to you
   without any thought that they are probably not attainable. _____

   _____

   _____

   _____

   _____

9. Do you prefer working for a large company or a small company?
   Why? _____

   _____

   _____

   _____

10. Any thoughts about going into business for yourself? _____

   _____

   _____

   _____

   _____

   _____

Set *Your* Career Goals

Now you can sit back and think about the type of position you should be looking for. Depending on your age, you may set one, two, or three goals. Everybody, however, should decide on the first goal—the next job. The younger person should set a stepping-stone goal that will lead to the ultimate goal—the position to be in at the apex of one's career.

In thinking of career goals, let your imagination run wild. Enter fantasy land and list the unattainable. Often those thoughts can be brought down to the world of reality and result in choosing a career field that does exist. Bob R. was dean of students at a well-known college. He did not enjoy the job and came to us for career direction as well as guidance in finding a new position. He had a law degree and had taught at college level. Practicing law interested him even less than the world of academia. We listed eighteen positions (there are more than thirty-five thousand known job titles) he could fill. Some of these were more attainable (practical) than others. Since Bob had a great need to be of service to others, we selected charity administration work as best fitting his strongest motivation. Actually, a major part of his dissatisfaction as dean of students was his repugnance at doing what he considered a disservice, such as inflicting penalties on troublemakers in the student body. Our marketing campaign resulted in Bob becoming the number-two man in a national charity organization.

Another example of reaching out to set career goals involved Joyce B., who had a degree in home economics and served as an adviser to the design engineering staff of a large appliance manufacturer. She represented the thinking of the housewife in the design or modification of the company's products. Although I had never heard of the title consumer affairs specialist, I suggested that Joyce enter the market as such. We designed a campaign aimed at manufacturers and retailers of consumer products. In just a few months she accepted a position as consumer affairs specialist with one of the largest supermarket chains. A few years later she became manager of their consumer services department. Today she is a partner in a consulting company specializing in consumer relationships. She has progressed with the consumer movement, which hardly existed when we mapped her career.

There are other stories of career changes, such as the certified public accountant who became an insurance broker, the housewares wholesaler who now markets people, the banker who changed to public relations, the salesman who became a buyer, and the buyer who switched to sales management.

Set *Practical* Goals Only

After going through all the steps necessary to *begin* thinking about career goals, you should find a way to measure both the practicality and the results of obtaining such a position. By results, I'm referring to your anticipated happiness in the new job. Will it fill your needs—your true motivations? Bob R. could undoubtedly make more money as an attorney than as a manager of a charity. A person with a need for security will not be a good entrepreneur. A high security need prevents the chief executive officer of a publicly held company from doing a good job. At times he or she must be able to risk the job and the company's money to further the company's growth.

To measure the practicality of obtaining the desired position, you should consider several factors. How big a market exists for such a position? The market for people who can sell is huge. Everybody wants to hire a good salesperson. Jobs selling insurance and in sales that pay commissions without draws, base salaries, or reimbursement of expenses are plentiful. On the other extreme, the number-one position as president or chief executive officer is obviously the least available.

Because so many persons not qualified for such a *top* position seem to fool themselves into thinking they are, it might be wise to bring up a few facts about how such positions are filled. Ideally, a firm will promote from within its own ranks. In this manner it gets a person who already knows almost everything about the company, its products, its markets, and its people. The firm also knows the person's strengths and weaknesses. Such a promotion improves morale and saves search and training expenses. If there is no qualified person, the firm will look on the outside, concentrating on either the president or the chief executive officer of a smaller company who is capable and desirous of an upward move, or the number-two person in a larger company who has been in training for the top job. An executive recruiter may or may not be used. The recruiter will conduct the search in more or less the same fashion to present only candidates perceived to be truly qualified.

A small or smaller company has more reason to promote from within. In fact it would rather promote from within the family that owns the company! The path to the top usually lies in starting your own business or being highly qualified, a good politician, and in the right place at the right time.

Assuming the market for the position under consideration is big enough, the next factor to consider is *your* chance of getting one of those jobs. How do you stack up against your competition? Rarely does a person looking for a new job get hired by a company that interviewed nobody else. Are you really qualified? Do your education, experience, and accomplishments prove those qualifications? Most important, can you sell yourself into such a position? It is a little-known fact that the better jobs do not go to the most qualified. They are awarded to the person who best sells his or her qualifications. This book discusses selling yourself *into* as well as in interviews.

Your final consideration in measuring the practicality of the selected job is an appraisal of your chances for success after you are in the new position. There is no reason why you should not look for a step up, including more authority and responsibility. But do not step too far. You should plan to make the big upward moves in your next company by earning promotions.

Salary was not discussed in setting goals and learning about yourself because salary is based on the position and its worth to the employers. After learning later in this book how to interview and negotiate, you will be able to think and talk salary, fringes, authority, responsibility, and possibly equity.

As soon as you have learned about yourself and set realistic career goals, you can start preparing your sales tools. Answering ads is both a sales tool and an important aid in preparing sales tools. Read about it in the next chapter.

3

The True Value
of Answering Ads

Don't ever let anyone convince you not to answer want ads. The very act of answering them is of great value, since it is like a practice interview in writing. By customizing each reply to your particular ability to fill the needs advertised, you are establishing sales facts about yourself more firmly in your own mind and will be better able to sell your qualifications in the interview. You will remember what you wrote if you take adequate time to compose each answer to fit the requirements as advertised.

By answering ads, you may also get new ideas about how your talents relate to today's markets. You may learn of things in your background that you did not realize were of true value today.

It has been said that many want ads do not represent true openings, as the jobs are already filled, and that companies use such ads just to prove they are complying with hiring regulations. This is undoubtedly true in some instances. I believe it to be especially true of ads run by government agencies. But, despite this and the fact that many of the better positions are not advertised, a big majority of the ads do reflect actual job openings. Isn't it best to cast your bait where the jobs are?

Avoid Common Ad-Answering Errors

Before we discuss *how* to answer ads, let us look into how *not* to. By avoiding the errors committed by almost everyone in answering ads, you will have a real edge over your competition. You will find that many of these ideas on how to answer ads are contrary to your present thinking; but believe me, they have been proved right in hundreds of cases. I am sure you will agree they make good common sense. By following them, you will have a better chance to get the right position with a good compensation package. I don't claim that these suggestions will produce results for an assembly-line worker. Rather, they are designed for executives of all levels.

Take Care with Blind Ads

Some caution is in order for blind ads. Obviously, you do not want to answer any ad that might possibly have been placed by your own employer. You can usually answer such an ad safely by using a friend's name and address. If you live in your own home, use a fake name and your own address. Answer such an ad this way *only* if you want to verify that it is your present company or if you are very interested in the position. There is one disadvantage to this method: If the employer does turn out to be other than your present one, it will create doubts in the mind of the interviewer when you properly identify yourself. But at least it may lead to an interview.

You can also play it safe by addressing your letter to the box number and the publication and writing in big letters on the envelope "DO NOT FORWARD IF THIS IS XYZ COMPANY." I have read that the laws of some states require newspapers and magazines to divulge names of companies placing blind ads. So far, however, I have never been able to find a state with such a law. In fact, the regional advertising manager of a well-known business paper tells me he has never heard of such regulations, and his region covers fourteen states.

Don't Rush Your Ad Replies

Another change in your thinking regarding ad answers concerns when to mail your reply. You should compose your answer as soon as possible but not mail it for four to seven days. Why? Primarily because,

I'm sorry to say, your answer will be competing with hundreds of others. Avoid the opening deluge of replies. At the same time give yourself a chance to improve the letter. Put it out of your mind for at least two days after writing it. This will allow you to make valid improvements later, as discussed on page 38.

How You Fit the Needs

How do you start your reply? What do you say in the first paragraph? Now you are about to learn the secret of selling yourself in ad answers and in interviews. The main reason you will be interviewed is the possibility that you can fill the bill. By the same token, you will be hired if, among other things, you are considered to be the most qualified to fill those needs. Therefore, attract attention with an opening that shows you fit the most important requirement.

Unlike most of the others who answer the ad, do not waste the valuable opening statement by saying that you are answering an ad of such and such a date in such and such a paper for such and such a position. If it is a blind ad, you can give all that information by putting the box number, the publication, and its address at the top of your reply as the address to which you are writing. If it is an open ad, you must still acknowledge it. For example, if you are answering an ad of February 3 in the *Wall Street Journal* for a controller, put

> Re: 2/3 WSJ ad
> CONTROLLER

in the upper right-hand corner of your letter. You don't need to give the year, since it will appear in the date of your letter. Surely, you can see how a reply that immediately gets down to showing how you qualify is superior to one that doesn't.

No Cover Letters, Please—Sales Letters Only

Should your ad answer really be a cover letter with which to send your resume? Absolutely not! In effect, every answer should be a sales letter that sells you as the one most qualified. You certainly can do that much better in a letter that emphasizes how you fit the specific requirements than in a preprinted resume. When looking for a job, you cannot afford the easy way out of writing cover letters. Everything you say or write should be aimed at selling yourself. This means you are continually proving you are the right person for each opening under discussion. Your particular talents of interest to Company A can be quite different from your other talents that impress Company B.

Send No Resume Unless . . .

Usually, you should *not* send a resume with ad answers. If a resume is not mentioned, do not send one. Don't even mention in your reply that you have one. If it is requested, send it with your sales-type reply only under certain conditions, one being that it fits the ad. When you wrote your resume, you carefully considered such aspects as your business history, accomplishments, and education. You included what you thought were your most important selling points. Perhaps you chose points A, B, C, D, and E. Now you are answering an ad calling for someone with experience in D, E, F, G, and H. Your resume doesn't show F, G, and H, though they are part of your ability/experience factor. Since the prospective employer's main use of each resume is weeding out unlikely applicants, you are automatically out. In a situation like this, you should sell yourself in a letter without a resume by covering your pertinent strong points. Or write a selling letter and a new selling resume that fits the requirements for the job.

If the ad asks for a resume, and your resume does fit the ad, send it along with a selling letter that calls attention to particular points in the ad and elaborates further on them.

Hold Back Your Salary History

Should you provide salary history if the ad so requests? Again, no! If you quote your present or latest earnings and they are less than your prospective employer was planning to pay, one of two things might happen—neither of them to your advantage. On the basis of money alone, you could be considered not truly qualified. If you fit the other qualifications you will probably be interviewed but offered less than the firm was planning to pay. If you show a salary higher than that intended, you will probably be considered overqualified. Thus, providing salary information can cost you either the job or a real increase in earnings.

Don't tell yourself you didn't want that interview anyway. Unless you are luckily overloaded with interviews, you want every one you can get. Even if you don't really want the job, practice interviews do wonders in preparing you for the real thing. You can afford to make your initial mistakes in such interviews. Also, in a case where the salary is low, you may possibly come across so well in the interview that you'll get the job at your price. And, as happens to a few of my clients each year, you may so impress the interviewer that the company will create a new position just for you.

I know of several situations in which the applicant received a starting base pay higher than the company had originally planned or budgeted. Without doubt, the best one relating to an ad answer involved Dave K. Many years ago Dave answered a blind ad for a controller's position. The ad specifically requested a resume and a salary history. Since Dave's resume fit the few requirements listed in the ad, he did send it with a sales-type letter that elaborated on his qualifications. Dave substantiated several measurable accomplishments with dollar figures and percentages but did not provide any salary information whatsoever.

Later he came to me with five different offers. One, I must admit, was absolutely no good. Two were, shall we say, just passing. Dave wanted to accept number four because it paid the most money—$25,000 a year. However, number five, the result of that ad answer, was in my detached, unemotional opinion the best for him. The offer was only $18,500, but I was confident Dave could get a higher starting salary by properly renegotiating with the relatively small company. It was obvious its two corporate officers truly wanted him above all other candidates for the job.

Dave agreed with me that the company and its officers represented a better long-range situation for him than the $25,000 offer if only he could talk them up a few thousand dollars. We felt that in a few years he would earn more than at the $25,000 company, be promoted from controller to treasurer, and possibly become at least a junior partner with a minority stock-holding position.

I suggested what Dave should say, and we role played it over and over. He was to ask for a $23,500 starting salary. The next day Dave phoned. "I never got to mention the twenty-three thousand, five hundred. I start Monday at twenty-seven thousand, five hundred!" I must confess I had not thought he would get that much; but I had been completely confident he would get more than originally offered, since he evidently fit the requirements almost perfectly and was liked personally.

The point of this story is that the company had planned to pay only $18,500. If Dave's answer had mentioned the $22,500 he was earning, it would have been discarded, as were the replies of those who indicated making more than $18,500. Today Dave is a stockholder and treasurer, just as we predicted.

Don't hurt your negotiating stance by giving a dollar answer to either salary history or salary requirements. Just ignore an ad request for either one. Your answer should do such a good job of showing how you meet their requirements that questions of salary will be deferred till the interview. However, you can reply to a question regarding your salary requirements by converting your answer to a sales pitch; for example, "While salary is not unimportant, my greater interest is to join a growing company where I can grow in income and responsibility as I help the company's growth." Of course, it will be obvious you are evading the salary issue. However, you will come across as an aggressive, hard worker with faith in yourself to do a good job. Also, you have not hurt your bargaining position by expressing a dollar figure that can be used to weed you out or start you at a salary that fits your expectations but is lower than the company had planned to pay before hearing from you.

Where is it written that a person earning $X in one job should be paid only $X or $X plus a small percentage increase in a new job? Isn't it to be expected that changes in responsibility, authority, industry, and location might require, or entitle a person to, a completely different pay scale? I have helped clients find positions that paid them many more dollars than the jobs they had left or lost. In 1978 one of my clients (an outplacement whose fee was paid by the company that fired him) went from $31,000 to $196,000. It entailed a complete change in location and industry. In fact, it involved a move to Tokyo—thus the great increase in pay. Costs there require a large compensation package. Actually, I estimate his new pay as being equivalent to $50,000 in the United States. That's a 61 percent increase over the job he lost.

Ask for the Order—the Interview!

How should you end your ad answer? With a call for action on the part of the advertiser. Your reply should sell you into an interview. Therefore, close the letter with a request for an interview. Don't hurt your positive sales approach with such qualifiers as "If you think I can do this job, please contact me for an interview at your convenience." Your letter should tell how you qualify. Don't add any ifs or buts. The interview will be at the convenience of the interviewer—the buyer— you are the seller, and in a job-search campaign it is almost always a buyer's market.

The Way to Get the Order

Now you have learned what not to do in answering ads. You also know the big secret—a good answer will sell the advertiser on your particular abilities and background to fill the specific needs. At this point, there is absolutely no interest in you other than the possibility that you can do a good job.

Sources of Ads

Let's discuss how to answer that ad in a step-by-step process. Start by looking for ads in the newspapers or trade journals that fit your market. The *Wall Street Journal* on weekdays, the Sunday *Chicago Tribune* and *New York Times* and the Sunday editions of your home-town paper or a newspaper in what you want to be your hometown are your best bets. Some trade journals in your industry may also have the ads you are seeking.

Classified Ads Can Pay Off

No matter how important you consider yourself, do not ignore the classified ads. I'm constantly amazed at the top-level or upper-level jobs cheaply advertised there. One client replied to the following ad, which appeared in the classified section of a Sunday metropolitan paper.

PRESIDENT

Wanted by housewares manufacturer.
Reply by resume to Personnel Mngr.
Box ABC 123

A prospective president should send a resume to personnel? My client followed my guidance regarding the submitting of resumes to ads placed by personnel departments. Send one with a sales-type letter—not a cover letter. If the ad does show some requirements and personnel wants a resume, rewrite your resume to fit the ad. It is very likely personnel won't interview anybody who doesn't submit a resume if one is requested.

The personnel manager spent only a few minutes with my client before taking him upstairs to meet the president, who was promoting himself to chairman of the board. My client was hired at $50,000 per year plus a bonus based on both sales and profits. Today he owns 50 percent of the stock, and the chairman has retired. All this from a one-inch-by-one-column ad in the classified section!

The classified pages are divided alphabetically according to job title or description. Before searching for the better ads, think of where you might fit. For example, a sales manager should look under S for sales and sales manager, E for executive, M for manager and marketing manager.

If you still doubt the possibility of finding a job from a classified ad, let me quote part of a letter I received from Tony C., a recruiter for a prestigious consulting firm: "The advice you gave me at our second meeting still amazes me." This advice was to answer classified as well as display ads. Tony saw one such ad listing four openings similar to what he was seeking and sent a letter describing himself and his qualifications. As a result, he found a position paying exactly $10,000 more than the one at his consulting firm.

Steps in Answering Ads

Now that you have found either classified or, preferably, display ads to answer, the fun begins. Cut the ads out of the paper, and, as soon as possible, sit down with them and an Ad Answer Work Sheet, as shown in figure 3. Fill out the work sheet in full, with special emphasis on the Requirements Expressed in Ad. After listing them, read the ad again to determine their relative importance, and rate them accordingly. If you have any doubts, the order in which they appear in the ad is often the best guide and may truly be in the order of importance to the advertiser.

Next, record your qualifications for each of the needs you meet. Don't be concerned about qualifications or experience you lack. There is no perfect person for any job. The advertiser is going to hire the person considered the most qualified. If you fit a majority of the listed requirements and are interested in the position, you should answer.

If You Fit All the Requirements

If you meet *all* the requirements, say so; but start with the most important one. Be sure to include measurable accomplishments, such as "Under my direction, sales of a slow, marginally profitable line went up 10 percent during my first year in charge. I not only boosted them another 40 percent in the next twelve months but also introduced economies in our sales approaches that actually cut sales costs 10 percent as volume went up."

Your next paragraph should positively state you fit *every* requirement advertised. Start each following paragraph by quoting each requirement. Don't be concerned if it is not a complete sentence. Just quote directly from the ad, underlining the quote. Then, in either outline or paragraph form, explicitly state how you fill that need. Add a final paragraph requesting an interview. It can be as simple as "May I have an interview? Please call or write." Again I remind you: Don't ever say "If you believe I fit. . . ."

If You Don't Meet All the Requirements

If your background does not fit all the requirements, you should still start the letter by showing how you can fill the one you selected on the work sheet as being the most important. Then, in the order in which you rated their importance to the advertiser, treat each of the other requirements that you personally fit.

Fig. 3

AD ANSWER WORK SHEET

Date of Ad _____ Publication _____

Ad Title _____ Company/Box No. _____

Your Analysis of Company (Size, Structure, etc.)_____

REQUIREMENTS EXPRESSED IN AD: * Rating	YOUR QUALIFICATIONS IN RELATION TO THE REQUIREMENTS:
1. ( )	
2. ( )	
3. ( )	
4. ( )	
5. ( )	
6. ( )	
7. ( )	
8. ( )	
9. ( )	
10. ( )	

* Rating: Show order of importance to the ADVERTISER--not to you,
           the applicant.

<u>CHECKLIST</u>

( )   Have you listed all advertised requirements?
( )   Have you related to the request for a resume as instructed
      by this book?
( )   Have you related to the request for salary requirements as
      instructed by this book?   <u>DO</u> <u>NOT</u> <u>INCLUDE</u> <u>CURRENT</u> <u>EARNINGS</u>
      <u>OR</u> <u>SALARY</u> <u>HISTORY</u>
( )   Have you attached a copy of your answer to this checklist?
( )   Have you shown related measurable accomplishments?

Play Back the Ad's Key Words

In each case, use the key words in the ad and show how well you meet the requirements. It is not enough to say you managed a manufacturing operation. Again, try to include measurable accomplishments, using percentages, dollars, or numbers.

Those key words are important. The advertiser thought them out carefully before placing the ad. The writer of the ad probably likes the sounds of his or her own words. If the advertiser gets more replies than expected, he or she may well turn them all over to a subordinate for the initial screening of applications. The subordinate will look for those buzz words. As I said before, your resume may not have the key words even though you do have the required experience. Such a resume would definitely cause you to be weeded out by a subordinate with hundreds of responses to select from.

Consider Replies Overnight Before Mailing

Answer the ad as soon as possible after first seeing it. Do it more or less as a rough draft. Put it away and don't even think about it for a few days. Three to six days later review your reply. Start by pretending you are the person who wrote the ad. Reread the ad carefully. Then read your reply asking yourself if it sells the writer to you—the advertiser. You are bound to find ways to improve your answer from the advertiser's point of view.

What Your Letter Should Look Like

Now you are ready to prepare a mailable answer. Your letter should be neat and error free. If at all possible, have it typed. If you can't type, hire somebody. Public stenographers are the best but also the most expensive. Perhaps you have a friend who can type for you. Visit the typing teacher at the nearest high school. Perhaps a student will want to make some extra money. Hand print a three-by-five-inch ad for a typist and put it on the bulletin board at your supermarket. The letter should be typed on a personal letterhead that shows your name, complete address, and phone number—don't forget the telephone area code. The monarch-size stationery, 7½ by 10 inches, is usually best for executives. Figures 4, 5, and 6 represent some sample letterheads and envelopes. Be sure to use white or off-white bond paper of average or better weight.

Write in Human-ese, Not Business-ese

In your ad answers, always try to be a human being rather than a self-important executive who writes in the language of business. Compose your letters as much as possible in the way you would talk face to face. Since you are writing about yourself, you must use the word *I,* but hold it to a minimum. Try not to start more than one paragraph with that overly used word. Don't say, "I successfully control all the finances of a major manufacturer." Instead, say, "As the chief financial officer of a major manufacturer, I was so successful in saving money that we now have a full-time investment staff under my direction."

Each ad answer should be about three-fourths of a page. Less than this means you did not put in the time and thought it deserves. Sometimes a one-and-a-half- or two-page reply is in order. Never go beyond two pages—it won't be read.

Customized Replies Pay Off

Yes, putting time into properly answering ads will pay off. A reply tailored to the ad will make you stand out above your competition. One month I received phone calls from four excited clients, who were more or less in seventh heaven. Each had responded to an ad and had been told that the reply was one of the few of more than one thousand that was being considered. To quote one advertiser: "So far, we've received an immense response numbering more than twelve hundred applicants. From these we *selected* a small percentage, including yours, that we hope may be properly qualified."

Three of those clients had interviews. Two received offers. One accepted the offer. Interestingly, the person who received the letter quoted above decided with me in advance he did not want the job. This was based on other factors mentioned in the letter. Because we both felt he needed some practice interviews, he went on the interview. His was the offer received and turned down.

Fig. 4

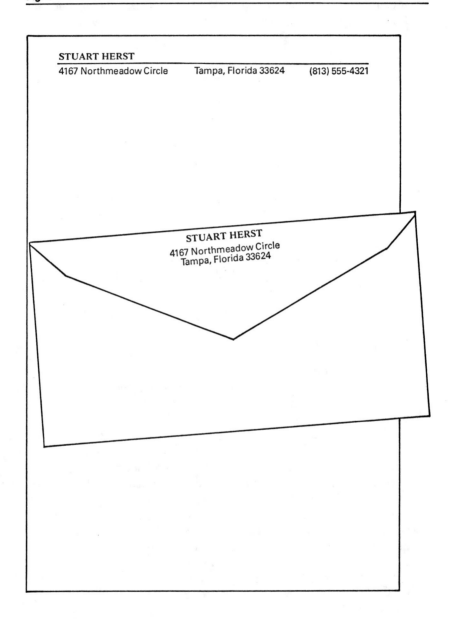

Fig. 5

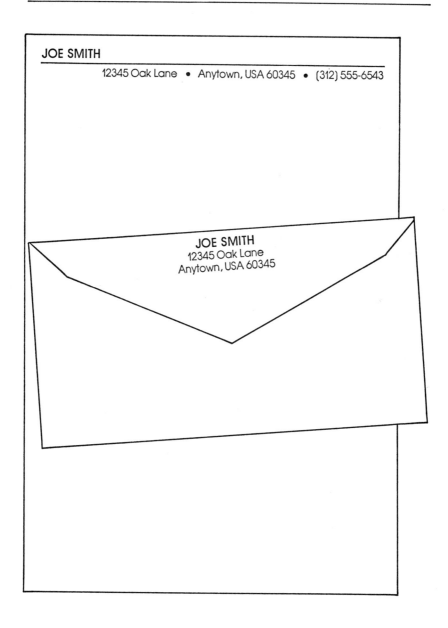

Fig. 6

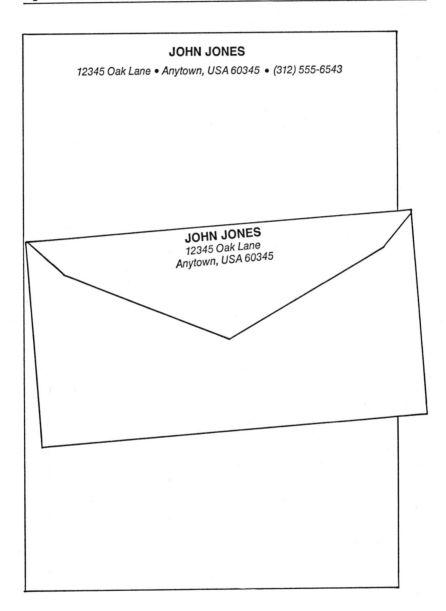

Think Beyond the Job Advertised

Although feeding back the advertised words is the name of the game in answering ads, do use your imagination. Remember the story of the boy who took the Boy Wanted sign out of the store window, handed it to the manager, and told him the sign was no longer needed, as he was the boy for the job. Whether open or blind, ads can give you an idea of how you can fit into a particular firm in a position other than the one advertised. The idea is worth a letter, a phone call, or a visit to the company.

Tony A. went to a specialized distributor and told the receptionist he was answering their ad. The boss came storming out and demanded to know how Tony had traced their blind ad. Tony pointed out that the ad referred to the unnamed company as the largest and most reliable distributor of a certain type of equipment in the Midwest. He told the company president it had to be that particular company. Needless to say, Tony was hired. After one month Tony was offered equity participation—40 percent of the corporation's stock.

Your Ad Answers Are Interviews in Writing— Good Practice

To summarize, you should answer any ad you seem to fit. Sell yourself as a person already proved capable of filling the needs advertised. Feed back the words used by the prospective employer. It is usually advisable to avoid sending a resume. Never give salary history unless your present or latest salary is just under or approaching the salary listed in the ad. Answer the ad like a human being who knows how to put the best foot forward. Always ask for interviews. Consider ad answers as "written interviews" that prepare you for the sessions that count.

Some of your better ad answers can be modified to fit the general sales letter you *should* send out. Chapter 4 tells you about this most important self-marketing technique.

4

The Sales Letter—
Your Most Important
Marketing Technique

A well-written sales letter mailed to carefully selected executives usually produces more interviews for the true executive than any other job-search technique. This does not mean you should ignore other methods. It means only that you cannot afford to omit this approach unless you have been offered a position that is too good to refuse. You will already have answered ads, made cold calls, met with or written to personal contacts, and probably written to your university and professional organizations before you get the sales letter in the mail. Your sales letter will, in a very punchy manner, *sell* your abilities to prospective employers. It tells them what you have done. Certain accomplishments are described with the strong suggestion that what you did for another company can also be done for the recipient of your letter.

Like the ad answer, it starts with an attention getter. The first paragraph should also tell what type of position you fit. Personally, I have never felt it necessary to state in the first or second paragraph that you are writing about a job with that particular firm. Your letter should be "salesy" enough to indicate that. Of course, as in the ad answer, you should close with a request for action—an interview.

Before writing a sales letter, you should answer several ads to gain practice in selling yourself and get new ideas on how you best fit the requirements of the current job market. In fact, there may be sentences or paragraphs in some of your ad answers that could well be adapted for, or inserted directly into, your sales letter.

As in answering ads, it is highly recommended that you avoid starting paragraphs with the word *I*. Use measurable accomplishments, showing dollars saved or earned, percentages, or just plain numbers. Quantify everything possible. Unless you are a Ph.D. applying for a teaching post at a university, compose your letter with short rather than long words and sentences. Make it easy to read and understand.

Study the Sample Sales Letters

Sample sales letters that have worked are shown in figures 7-14. Of course, parts of the letters and all the individual names have been changed. They have been included not to be copied but to give you ideas on how to compose your letter. While these are all one page in length, a sales letter of one and a half or two pages would also be satisfactory. Don't write three pages or more. Most executives won't want to devote much time to reading an unsolicited letter from a stranger.

Your sales letter is worthy of considerable time and thought in its preparation. Your first draft (after answering ads) should be put aside for a few days and read later when your mind will be clearer and improvements can be made. In that time work on compiling the list of managers and firms to whom to send the letter. Obviously, your letter should be aimed at this list.

Sometimes it is advisable to have more than one letter and one list. For example, if you have a good background in the machine tool industry, one letter restricted to machine tool manufacturers should specifically mention your work in that field, while another letter to manufacturers in general should not refer to machine tools but should emphasize how you would fit into any manufacturing company.

Don't Reveal Too Much in the Sales Letter

Unlike a resume, your sales letter should not mention company names and usually should not show job titles. It is possible that a

Fig. 7   A Salesman's Sales Letter

_____

ALLEN L. LEWIS

149 Duckbill Lane . . . Houston, Texas   77014 . . . (713) 555-2230

Date

Name, Title
Company
Street Address
City, State, Zip Code

Dear _____:

Can I interest you in an award-winning, hardworking sales manager/
salesman? My successful performance in both categories last year
won me a promotion to a regional sales managership in a company
that has been cutting back on its sales and sales-management
personnel.

When my region was ordered to increase sales of one product line
15% in just three months, we were able to boost sales 71%. I
analyzed past sales and then developed specialized marketing techniques, taught them to my people, and brought in these increases from
both old and new customers, including competitive distributors
and types of accounts not previously sold.

Since receiving my degree, I have been with only one company. In
that time I have worked myself up from a position as a sales trainee
to that of a salesman and a sales manager.

In addition to training and managing salespeople, I have supervised
a local operation in which I was able to cut costs $31,000 per year.
This shows you that I'm a cost-and-profit-conscious sales manager/
salesman.

An interview is requested so I can prove my sales ability to you.
The sale I want to make will put me on your sales team.

Sincerely,

Allen L. Lewis

Fig. 8   A Personalized Sales Letter for Competitors of Present Employer

BERTRAM P. LANGLEY

9201 W. 34th Street   St. Louis, Missouri 63121   (314) 555-9211

Date

Name, Title
Company
Street Address
City, State, Zip Code

Dear _____:

An engineering manager, I'm also the administrative, systems, and product planner for a leading control-systems manufacturer. Our computer and noncomputer control systems are supplied to electric utilities, gas and oil pipeline companies, and process industries, such as water- and wastewater-treatment plants.

I have helped establish two separate companies engaged in the same fields as yours. These companies have become leaders. My abilities in developing and managing an engineering department, establishing test facilities, customer sales and contracts, contract negotiation, new-product introductions, improving old products, analyzing competitive products, long-range planning, and providing technical and management expertise for manufacturers of engineered products or providers of technical services can be of value to you.

For my present employer, Automation Industries, a subsidiary of Controls Corp., the groups I formed are responsible for the manufacturing, engineering, market support, and customer requirements of product lines whose volume increased fivefold.

A BSEE, I also earned a BS in math. I'm writing to you, as I believe that the _____ has all the ingredients and the potential of being the leader in the control-systems market. With my experience and background, I could help your company reach this goal. I would appreciate it if you would keep this information confidential.

An interview is requested to really show you my potential with your firm.

Sincerely,

Bertram P. Langley

Fig. 9   An Able Woman's Sales Letter

ROSEMARY MANN
1233 South 3rd St.
Williamsville, N.Y. 14221
(716) 555-5287

Date

Name, Title
Company
Street Address
City, State, Zip Code

Dear _____:

Presently a department head in a large insurance company, I have
the managerial experience, capabilities, and ambition to progress
in the management ranks of a company like yours. I can fit into
your organization and your industry.

You will find me creative and intelligent. I personally planned
and developed this department when given the challenge of creating
the methods and procedures required to control a completely new
brokerage operation. We now service all field personnel, brokers,
and policyholders. I report to the chief operating officer and
interface with all department heads and almost all employees of
our company, as well as our brokers and their staffs and clients.

Present and previous administrative-management experience includes
hiring, training, operational analyses, writing employee manuals,
establishing wage classifications, travel to field offices, sales,
and corporate-image promotion. In addition to a degree,* I have
taken five management-development seminars at the University of
Michigan.

Married and the mother of two teenagers, I am free to travel and
relocate. Obviously, I am interested in career advancement. I
enjoy the challenge of the business world.

May I have an interview?

Sincerely,

Rosemary Mann

*Her degree is not related to the business world and therefore not named here.

Fig. 10   An Air Force Officer's Sales Letter

PAUL GREEN

1605 E. Wells Street * Chicago, Illinois 60651 * (312) 555-8513

Date

Name, Title
Company
Street Address
City, State, Zip Code

Dear _____:

Don't throw this letter away just because I've been an air force
officer 99% of my adult life. My education and career history
point at my value to your organization as a consultant ... in
communications. Communications can be technical or face-to-face.

On the technical side, in solving problems and streamlining systems,
I have been operations and administrative head of radio, teletype,
and telephone communications networks that serve customers worldwide.

Additional background includes directing the Air Force Academy's
Language Laboratory and serving as Budget Administrator of its
Department of Foreign Languages. I have built three civilian
apartment buildings and a $1,500,000 air force installation.

As to face-to-face communications, I have coordinated international
functions, briefed high-ranking dignitaries of many nations, and
been involved with protocol activities at international, social,
and business levels. Besides teaching German, political geography,
and business administration at three universities, I've written a
three-volume text and laboratory manual on the German language.
This work is now used by many colleges.

Education: All but the dissertation for a PhD in Institutional
Management and Business Administration, an MBA in Industrial
Management, a BS in Education, and a BA in Economics and Political
Science. In addition, I have taken many courses in law, elec-
tronics, communications, human relations, teaching, management,
and counseling.

This wide background makes me feel I can fit into your firm. I
would like to meet with you or a member of your staff to discuss
the ways in which I could best serve your company.

Sincerely,

Paul Green

P.S. Highest security clearances available. I'm willing to travel
     or relocate anywhere in the world.

Fig. 11   An Advertising Woman's "Advertisement"

JUDY SMITH
3225 Central Avenue
Washington, D.C. 20031
(202) 555-3607

Date

Name, Title
Company
Street Address
City, State, Zip Code

Dear _____:

Advertising and public- and customer-relations management is a wide
field requiring a true professional. My diversity of experience
qualifies me to inquire about a position with your firm. While with
an ad agency, I supervised PR and advertising for many clients,
including manufacturers of consumed goods, consumer articles, and
capital equipment. I also serviced such organizations as professional groups, banks, and insurance carriers.

Presently with a multinational service organization as Manager of
Advertising, PR, and Publications, I constantly strive to maintain
and improve its corporate image for the entire area it services, as
well as for its own employees and franchisees. It is my privilege
to head our in-house ad agency and to work with the outside agency.
Besides being editor/publisher of the house organ, I personally
create or supervise preparation of films, speeches, and all kinds
of sales and advertising material. I've won some top awards,
but more important, have continually increased our sales and
improved our customer relations.

In this position I have the opportunity to counsel other divisions
or departments on promotions, training, sales materials, recruiting,
purchasing, and communications.

So, why this letter? I can't achieve all I'd like to with my present
company. I believe I can do more for one like yours. May I have an
interview?

Sincerely,

Judy Smith

P.S. Age 30 ... MA and BA in English ... Available to travel and
     relocate.

Fig. 12   An Unusual Approach for an Unusual Situation

RUDOLPH H. HELLER

1244 S. State Street * Chicago, Illinois 60601 * (312) 555-6122

Date

Name, Title
Company
Street Address
City, State, Zip Code

Dear _____:

If I were to run an Executive Available ad, here is what it would
say:

INTERNATIONAL TAX MANAGER
ACCOUNTING MANAGEMENT

    International tax specialist who can advise and moni-
tor intercompany and international transactions to
determine both U.S. and foreign tax impact and compliance requirements. Fully capable of handling U.S. tax
audits of foreign-related operations and foreign-
country audits of both foreign and domestic activities.
Can obtain proper foreign-tax credits. Monitors tax
laws. Suggests accounting procedures and methods to
minimize foreign and U.S. taxes on international income.

I have particular expertise in Western European tax laws. As a
former Deputy District Director of the West German "IRS," I have
made decisions and given advice on international tax matters.
This covered foreign and domestic taxes on corporations and individuals, including income, trade, sales, and value-added taxes.
I'm very familiar with the U.S. Tax Reform Act of 1976.

A degreed attorney, I also have the equivalent of a CPA. In fact,
I lived five years in the U.S. as an auditor for a Big 8 CPA firm
and as the Chief Accountant of a publishing company. I'm fluent
in English and German, can read and speak French adequately to do
the job, and am so-so with Italian.

May we meet to discuss how I can help your company take the right
accounting steps to save money on international taxes? I'm looking
for full-time employment in accounting or tax management in both a
doer and an advisory capacity.

Sincerely,

Rudolph H. Heller

Fig. 13 A Banker's Sales Letter

JOHN P. BANKER

1919 West 19th Court * Owensboro, Kentucky 42301 * (502) 555-7212

Date

Name, Title
Company
Street Address
City, State, Zip Code

Dear _____:

I have two reasons for writing to the top . . . to you.

First, as Chairman of the Board you, more than anyone else in your
organization, know the needs for growth. You are the one who established the criteria for senior management personnel in your bank.

Second, my experience and talents can help fill these needs. As a
bank president for fifteen years, my accomplishments include:

    -- increasing resources of one bank 250% and of a much
       larger bank 60%;
    -- improving profit percentages considerably in excess
       of resource growth;
    -- developing loyal staffs through incentive programs,
       simultaneously creating a strong, cooperative spirit;
    -- modernizing all operating procedures, thereby cutting
       costs;
    -- developing community confidence through successful
       public relations programs;
    -- counteracting community skepticism in a situation of
       absentee bank management.

The application of professional management methods in working with
personnel, coupled with my knowledge of every phase of banking from
the teller's cage to the Board of Directors, is the tool of success.
My contacts with people and the development of productive personal
relationships are among my major strengths.

Shouldn't we meet to discuss how I can help your bank better serve
its depositors and the community?

I look forward to hearing from you soon.

Sincerely,

John P. Banker

Fig. 14   Hiding Behind a Friend

DONALD FISHER

1115 North Kent Avenue * Pasadena, California 91140 * (213) 555-2270

Date

Name, Title
Company
Street Address
City, State, Zip Code

Dear _____:

Are you interested in a capable executive in your industry? I'm
writing about a man with more than twenty years of progress and
success in the formulation and production of organic pigments
and related products. At present he enjoys complete responsibility
for profit and loss in a facility with sales over $40,000,000.
This covers all that operations management entails, including manufacturing, materials, R & D, engineering, and personnel, plus the
management of accounting and budgets.

In addition to an MBA in Production Management, he has a BS in
Chemistry, and all but a thesis for an MS in Industrial Chemistry.
Almost a continuous student, he has taken many industry courses
in research, manufacturing, and general management.

His writings have been published, and he has five chemical proces-
sing patents.

Your products are known to him. You probably know of him. He can
produce efficiently and profitably for you. His reasons for desiring a change will make sense to you. One short meeting will answer
your questions as to how he would be a true asset for _____.

A letter will arrange that meeting. Please let me hear from you.
I will make the necessary arrangements.

All replies will be answered.

Sincerely,

Donald Fisher

prospective employer may have negative feelings about your company. Unless it is really looked up to as a good training ground for your specialty, you are probably better off not calling attention to it in the sales letter. Omit job titles because an impressive one can preclude you from an interview involving a better job that doesn't sound so impressive. If you are not employed, don't say so. Your letter should give the impression that you are seeking a job change.

Never Send a Resume with a Sales Letter

Your resume does *not* go with the sales letter to prospective employers. As already explained in this book, resumes are primarily used as a screening device to weed people out. Most resumes show titles and companies—an important factor in that process.

Some people mark the envelope "Personal and Confidential" in the hope the letter will get past the screening efforts of a secretary and be opened and read by the executive to whom it is addressed. Our experience over the years has not confirmed this.

However, if you are a lawyer, I suggest you put "Attorney at Law" under your name on the envelope but not on your letterhead. If you feel you want to use it, "Personal and Confidential" can be typed or rubber-stamped—not printed—on the envelope.

Examples of the Sales Letter's Impact

Occasionally, clients have received negative replies to ad answers but have ended up having interviews with the same companies as a result of their sales letters. Timing and just plain luck can affect the impact of a sales letter. About once a year I receive a phone call from a client long established in the position we found together. He or she calls to tell me about receiving a phone call or letter as a result of a sales letter of many months or even a few years ago. It seems the original letter was kept on file and *now* the prospective employer wants to talk. Invariably, I tell the client to go to the interview no matter how good the present job is. In almost half the cases, the client again advances his or her career by accepting a new and better position.

Many sales letters are forwarded to other companies or to executive searchers. Clients often get called for interviews by companies they have not approached. Almost all such interviews are the result of forwarded sales letters.

Gus P. had sent his resume to several executive searchers before becoming my client but had got nowhere. However, almost immediately after his sales letter went out, he was contacted by one of those searchers, who had been looking for three months for a person with the particular expertise that Gus possessed. The searcher had received the letter through a corporate client to whom Gus had written. Gus was intelligent enough not to hurt the searcher's feelings by revealing that he had previously sent a resume. After one interview with the searcher and two with the company, Gus was hired. The sales letter had succeeded in opening the door where the resume had failed.

Carl S. received a negative form letter from a personnel vice-president as the result of a sales letter addressed to the company president. One week later the vice-president phoned, saying the president wanted Carl to be interviewed. At the interview Carl was shown a sales letter that he had written to one of the president's friends, who had forwarded it directly to the president with a note that Carl sounded like the man the company needed to start a new product line previously discussed. Carl got the job. We'll never know whether the vice-president realized he had once turned Carl down. Carl has been there several years now and has been advised not to bring it up.

What You Can Expect from Your Sales Letter

How many replies and interviews should your sales letter generate? No single figure can answer that question. A letter looking for a chief executive officer position will draw fewer positives than one seeking an interview for a product-management slot. My all-time record was a 55 percent return for a young man with a brand new M.B.A. He had a job driving a forklift truck in a large warehouse, but the letter implied he was looking for his first job.

The economic conditions affect the response ratio. If the stock market falls sharply today, so will the responses on letters mailed today or yesterday.

Any letter that does not produce at least a 3 percent positive response should be looked at very carefully for needed revision.

Your sales letter should be on the same monarch-size stationery as that used in answering ads. The letterhead should have your name, address, and phone number to make it easy for the company to reach you.

Look upon the sales letter as your primary marketing technique. It succeeds because somewhere there is a company that can use your particular abilities. Perhaps it doesn't even know it needs somebody like you till your letter arrives! Many people get jobs that did not exist before the sales letter planted the idea. Be assured that one of the best jobs you can get is one that the company creates for you.

Your Mailing List

Compiling your mailing list is necessarily time consuming if done right. To begin, you must study yourself (phase one) and select the industries in which you feel you belong and decide in what size company you would be happy.

In selecting industries, you will do best with a copy of the government's *Standard Industrial Classification Manual,* which is available in almost all libraries. At the present time the 1972 edition is the most current. This book assigns a four-digit standard industrial classification (SIC) number to every industry, including not-for-profit associations and government agencies. Proper use of this book will not only make it impossible for you to miss an industry related to your background but also start you on the path of locating the firms within those industries.

If you begin by carefully reading every word in the manual's table of contents, you will hit every industry that interests you and can possibly use your talents. Read the short description shown for each industry and record the two-digit numbers representing all those in which you feel you would want or could get a job. For instance, a civil engineer could fit in with certain companies engaged in agriculture, mining, building and road construction, some manufacturing, or engineering services, to name just a few.

Then turn to the pages indicated in the table of contents for your two-digit numbers. Opening to the first page shown, you will find descriptions and examples of products or services falling under that major group. Record the four-digit numbers representing the industries you select as best fitting your career plans.

Your library will also have a copy (current, I trust) of the *Dun & Bradstreet Million Dollar Directory,* which is advertised as listing every company with a net worth of a million dollars or more. By using the section headed "Business by Product Classification," you can find every company fitting the SIC codes you have chosen. The listing in this section shows names and addresses only. The large white-page section of the book will later be used to look up your selected companies to get the all-important name and title of the person to whom you want to address your sales letter. You will also find in this section useful additional information on those companies that you may want to record.

To save time and avoid errors, photocopy pages of the "Business by Product Classification" section. Cut out the names and addresses of particularly appealing companies and paste or cellophane tape them to individual three-by-five-inch cards. After putting them in alphabetical order, remove any duplicates. One company may be listed under as many as six SICs. Only one letter should go to a company at any one address.

With the cards alphabetized, you can leaf through the book in proper order—by name rather than by SIC number. Above the company's name on the card, legibly print the name and title of the executive you want to get your letter.

Note the sample three-by-five-inch card that follows.

```
Thomas P. Simms, President
ABC Corporation
456 N. Seventh Street
Chicago, IL  60608

Elect. Connectors

                   50/1000
```

Good sales letters are personalized. You should not write to:

President
ABC Corp.
456 N. 7th St.
Chicago, IL 60608

Dear Mr. President:

Instead, your letter should be addressed to:

Mr. Thomas P. Simms, President
ABC Corporation
456 N. Seventh Street
Chicago, IL 60608

Dear Mr. Simms:

To appear knowledgeable in case the response to your letter is a phone call, summarize certain facts about a company and its products on each card—the figures 50/1000 on the sample tell you the company has a sales volume of $50 million and 1,000 employees—and keep the cards in alphabetical order near your phone for ready reference. Other uses of the cards will be explained in chapter 6.

Your mailing list should never be less than 500. A mailing of 1,000 is much better. Without getting into the reasoning, you should know that a positive return of 5 on a mailing of 100 would result in *more* than 25 positives with the mailing of the same letter at the same time to 500 managers.

Address Sales Letter to Proper Officer

Selecting the right person to receive your letter is just as important as selecting the company. Unless you are looking for a personnel job, do not write to the personnel department. Address your letter to the person you think would most likely be your boss. If in doubt, write to his or her superior. For consideration as a regional sales manager, you should send the letter to the vice-president in charge of sales or marketing. If you are after the top sales management position, write to a senior or executive vice-president. Write to the president only if it is a smaller company or you just can't figure out who really should receive your letter. All too often letters to the president go directly to the personnel department without the president's seeing them.

The creation of a mailing list certainly sounds like a lot of work. It is, but it is important. You and only you selected the companies and the individuals on your list. That means your letter will not go to companies for whom you would not want to work. It won't go to localities where you don't want to live. In doing all that work, you familiarized yourself with the industries, your prospective employer's size and products or services, and, to some extent, the competition. Of course, you will do much more research on each company before your interviews. More on that later.

Typed Letters Pull More Than Printed Ones

Now that you have your stationery, a mailing list, and a punchy sales letter, you must find a service to prepare the letters. Your first choice (and most expensive) is a secretarial or letter service that uses word processors that automatically type each letter. Using the same machine or the same type and ribbon, the service can type in the name, title, company, address, and salutation so your letter looks just like what it is—an individually typed personalized message. There are printers who can print letters typewriter style and type-match the heading to the body; however, with effort, a distinction can be made between the two. Therefore, although this method is cheaper and faster, do not go this route without first seeing some samples. Then insist on a sample of *your* letter before the order is run.

Sign Each Letter—Personalize, Personalize, Personalize

You should sign the letters yourself. Any printed signature looks just like it really is—artificial. Mail the letters from your post office. Put individual stamps on them. The larger commemorative stamps will also help personalize your mailing. Never use a postage meter. You would like each of your readers to think you wrote that letter for and to him or her alone. At the very least, the recipient should feel that you put out only a few letters and he or she was one of the select few.

Avoid Holidays

Since Monday is an executive's busy day, mail the letters then so they will arrive on Tuesday, Wednesday, or Thursday. The date shown on the letters should be that of the mailing.

Don't do a mailing during a week shortened by a holiday. In a short week following or preceding a long weekend, the recipient is going to pay attention to routine and emergency company matters rather than to unsolicited letters. Of course, you should not mail sales letters between Christmas and New Year's. In fact, most companies wind down so much then that I usually prohibit client mailings from about December 15 to about January 10.

If you have 700 or more letters (you should try for 1,000), send only half in your first mailing. The response you receive may give you some ideas for slight improvements before you mail the second half.

Mailing a few each week is not to your advantage. Several inquiries from a large mailing will make you hold your head higher and do a better job in handling the responses and the interviews. It is much better to have to choose between offers as soon as possible than to have no offers. Many clients have asked me to work out their priorities because they have had too many replies to handle!

That is a problem I wish for my readers as well.

5

Preparation and Use of Your Resume

Without a doubt, resumes are the most misused, overused, abused, and misunderstood tools in the world. Certainly, as said elsewhere in this book, they have caused more lost interviews for job searchers than they have opened interviewers' doors. Why? Because no resume aimed at selling a person's particular abilities can fit an interviewer's needs perfectly unless the writer of the resume knows exactly the qualifications desired. Only then can the writer design a selling resume that does fit the job.

Try Not to Use Your Resume

Please do not forget one most important fact: Resumes are used by prospective employers to weed people out so they can devote their time to interviewing those candidates who appear on paper as the most qualified to fill the requirements.

Resumes, I repeat, are also used as crutches by the job hunter and the person with the power to hire. All too often, the job hunter, instead of highlighting particular talents that fit a particular job opening, will let the resume do the talking. If the resume passes the interviewer's screening, it is then used as a basis for questioning during the interview. The interviewer is holding all the cards, including those of the applicant, who has turned them over in the form of a resume.

Try to use your resume very sparingly. I have worked for only a few firms in my life, but none of my employers ever saw a resume of mine. In fact, looking back, I now realize I never used a resume as part of my job searches.

When starting in this field, I decided it would be wise to get several practice interviews so I could test my theories and be better able to coach my clients on interviewing techniques. I got those interviews by answering ads, using personal contacts, and making calls on likely employers. I did not use a resume either to get the interview or during the interview.

But I did make up one resume as a test. I sent it to a professional organization of which I was a member. For ten dollars, I could place a position or job wanted ad in its monthly magazine and have my resume kept on file for six months in case I might fit any inquiries. I heard nothing for seven months. Then one evening I received a phone call telling me I was no longer being considered for the position of executive vice-president of the organization. You guessed it! The caller was a member of the board of the organization that took my ten dollars. My resume had been a failure.

So, if resumes don't work, why prepare one? To begin with, the thought and introspection you put into writing your resume will help you sell yourself by phone, in ad answers, and in interviews. This goes back to phase one—learn the product. You should also make up a resume because there are times or places where they must be available or should be used. More on that later.

You should use professional help with a resume if you think it will improve it or your job-search campaign, but only after you have really studied yourself and actually prepared a resume outline.

How to Write a Resume

Start out by listing your jobs. Put on paper each company you have worked for, your various job titles or functions, a short description of your duties, and the years spent in each job. Don't worry about exact dates. At the executive level, years are enough.

Next, record your accomplishments—tell either how your actions made it possible for the company to make or save money or how they actually made or saved dollars. Quantify these accomplishments into dollars, percentages, or other numbers. These are the selling points that will make somebody hire you. Your next employer is looking for profit producers, problem solvers—the person who can do a good job.

Perhaps you can record accomplishments best if you divide each one into three parts. Begin with a description of the problem that existed. Then tell what you did to solve the problem. Finally, outline the positive results that came from your approach to the problem. You need not include these steps in your resume. I have suggested them as a method enabling you to think out your accomplishments in a logical manner.

Now that you have done all that writing, put it aside for one or two days. When you study it later, you will find things to add to it. You'll probably also make some corrections and improvements.

Then write your resume or work it out with a professional. There are as many forms a resume can take as there are people who have given it thought. I am now going to give you the benefit of my thoughts, which have been tested and revised for more than a decade in helping hundreds of clients with their resumes.

Don't Tell All in a Resume

As in the discussion of how to answer ads, let us start with what *not* to do. Do not waste your time and the reader's by printing "Resume" at the top. A good resume comes across as a resume at first glance.

Don't ever mention references. If they are wanted, they will be requested. You certainly don't want your references checked unless you have a genuine interest in the position. The people you use as references, as described elsewhere in this book, should not be abused by being used too often.

Please, no picture. It's childish. Also, the person who sees it may not like the way you part your hair, or have some other subconscious quirk involving your appearance that rules you out.

Salary or compensation package is another no-no. Why hurt your bargaining power? Why eliminate yourself from consideration as being too cheap or too expensive? In either case, the interview would be good practice for you, and the remuneration could possibly be adjusted after it is found that you are right for the job and the job is right for you.

If you are overweight, too short, lack a college degree, or have other limiting factors, don't show them. I never put weight and height in a resume except for a male client who has it all well put together in a six-foot-plus frame. If the client is divorced, I put single, as that is the person's real status at the time the resume is written. Being single can be a plus if your resume also says you are free to travel extensively and put in longer hours.

All these caveats are simply telling you not to put too much in your resume. Use only those facts you want known. Give only enough information to get an interview. This does not include facts about your spouse, the names and ages of your children, your date of birth, or your social security number.

If you have one or more college degrees, don't waste space and time saying you are a high school graduate. Your military service should be mentioned but not in any detail unless you did something in uniform that makes you a better person for the job.

Do not play up your hobbies. You are going to be hired to work, not play. I personally know two highly successful businessmen who refuse to hire people who play golf! Their belief is that golfers live and breathe golf. They believe a golfer thinks of golf instead of how to increase profits. However, saying you enjoy jogging, swimming, or tennis shows you are vigorously healthy.

Study These Sample Resumes

Figure 15 is a sample resume. Note that it shows a telephone number. I have seen many without phone numbers. Since such an omission makes it difficult for the prospective employer to contact you in a hurry, your competition for the job will probably be called instead.

The heading shows the type of position our Mr. Sweet can fill. He is searching for a job in general management but does not pin the title of president or executive vice-president on himself.

Mike M. worked for me in the fifties as a salesman and later as a regional sales manager. In 1972 he phoned for advice in finding a new job. At my request he sent me his resume. I told him to rewrite it with only one simple change. I wanted him to drop the heading Vice-President/Sales and substitute Sales Management. He fought the idea, telling me that he had been promoted to VP/Sales after I had left and he would not consider a step downward. I tried to convince him that a title was not as important as a position he would really enjoy and that paid good money and offered a real potential for growth. I failed to convince him. Nine months later Mike phoned again. His resume, which I had told him how *not* to use, had not produced one interview. He then agreed to change the resume to Sales Management, add one year to his age, and use the sales-letter technique. He accepted an offer as a sales vice-president five weeks later.

Most other sample resumes have brief paragraphs directly under the heading. (See figure 16.) This is a combined attention getter and summary of the individual's main selling points.

Next comes business experience, business history, career, or any such heading you want to give it. Please notice that a company is listed only once, no matter how many different positions were held there. Listing a company or a division again and again can plant the thought that the applicant is a job hopper. In fact, Sweet had one job that lasted only three months. But it is not shown on the resume!

Under each job title there should be a description of the functions, plus, if possible, measurable accomplishments. You can devote less and less space to the earlier jobs or to those not relating to the position desired.

Education is next in Mr. Sweet's resume. Had his education been a very important element qualifying him for the position, I would have put the education section ahead of the business background. For example, one of my clients who had a B.S. in Science, an M.S. in Chemistry, and a Ph.D. in Physics was seeking a management niche in research and development. The degrees, in his opinion and mine, outweighed his business experience to date. We put them up front, where they would catch attention.

The listing of military experience should be held to a minimum unless it helps sell the applicant. However, it should go into your resume if it is an important part of your history. Furthermore, it could leave a time gap if omitted.

A listing of any patents or publications could go next.

This leads us to the personal section. As said earlier, do not "let it

Fig. 15

CHARLES S. SWEET
123 Fourth Street * * * Tampa, Florida 33640 * * * (813) 555-6023

G E N E R A L   M A N A G E M E N T
M A N U F A C T U R I N G

Able, experienced manager who can and has assumed complete
responsibility of autonomous manufacturing divisions . . . turned
losses into profits. Registered Professional Engineer.

Functions performed include

-- Group Vice-President	-- 3,500 employees
-- General Manager	-- 2,500 employees
-- Manufacturing Manager	-- 2,000 employees
-- Plant Manager	-- 300 employees

CAREER:

ABC, INC.   1970-Present
Tampa, Florida
Group Vice-President, 1976-Present
Operate eight divisions with eighteen plants and 3,500 employees.
Improved ROI from 7.3% to 13.8%. Asset base reduced through
inventory management, receivables control, and effective capital
investment. Brought two divisions from losses to profits.
Introduced new products, including truck-mounted crane, mobile work
platforms, water-system expansion tank, swing hoists, and vibratory
rollers that generated over $3,000,000 in profitable sales.
General Manager, A-B Division, 1972-76
VP, Manufacturing, A-B Division, 1970-72
Built, staffed, and managed new plant. Produced profits in less
than 12 months of operation. Assumed complete P & L responsibilities, including management of sales and marketing.
Earned 30% pretax profits in 1976.

XYZ CO.   1965-1970
Springfield, Ohio
Plant Manager
Responsible for manufacturing, materials, inventory control, EDP,
industrial relations, manufacturing engineering, and warehousing.
Significant Accomplishments:
* Increased production 33% with same supervisory force.
* Determined site location for new factory. Directed refur-
    bishing of old building and start-up. Completed on schedule.
* Researched, planned, and installed two new methods of
    manufacturing that reduced labor costs 26%.

CHARLES S. SWEET   PAGE TWO

* Was senior company representative at labor negotiations for
  seven contracts. Only two strikes of one-week duration.
* Established centralized forecasting of material requirements,
  reducing obsolete material by 42%.

DEF CO.   1949-1965
Various locations
          Manager, Test Systems Engineering, Cincinnati, 1959-65
          Quality Control, Engineer, Large Engine Department,
              Cleveland, 1953-59
          Manufacturing Training Program, 1953
          Mechanical Design Engineer, 1949-52
Top position involved supervising four engineers in designing,
producing, and operating jet-engine test facilities. QC work with
Minuteman rocket. Manufacturing Training Program in three years
of night school at the graduate·level plus six full-time work
assignments aimed at creating well-rounded manufacturing managers.

EDUCATION:
BS, Mechanical Engineering, University of Wisconsin, 1946
Several manufacturing management courses taken (or taught) at
   Wharton, DEF Co., and American Management Association
Registered Professional Engineer

MILITARY:
U. S. NAVY   Repair Officer   1946-1949

PERSONAL DATA:
Age 53   Married, Three children
Available to travel, relocate

Past and present memberships:
   -- American Management Associations
   -- American Institute of Steel Engineers
   -- Society of Automotive Engineers

   Board member of several civic organizations

Fig. 16   A Marketing/Sales Manager's Resume

JACK B. SMITH
10 SOUTH MAIN STREET
CINCINNATI, OHIO 45320
(513)555-2131

S A L E S/M A R K E T I N G   M A N A G E M E N T

Wide international and domestic experience in marketing and marketing-services management; sales, sales training, and sales management; new-product development and introduction.

Successful background in supervising direct-mail advertising, advertising agency, sales-training consultants, salesmen, technical specialists, as well as worldwide sales meetings of over 350 <u>over quota</u> achievers.

A capable executive who can set sales goals and cost budgets and produce the results as planned . . . or plan all phases of business organization for growth and profit for both the short and long term.

<u>CAREER:</u> ALPHA INTERNATIONAL, INC.   1972-Present
          Cincinnati, Ohio

          <u>Director, Product and Business Planning, 1977-Present</u>
          Created firm's internationally oriented product-develop-
          ment program. In one year launched 30 new products in
          four broad product areas. Developed first long-range
          international product-and-business plan, involving
          finance, manpower, and marketing strategies.
          <u>Manager, Marketing Services, 1976</u>
          <u>Marketing Manager, 1972-76</u>
          By creating complete operational packages combining sales,
          advertising, sales materials, technical training instruc-
          tions, and sales training programs, achieved all sales/
          profit objectives on a controlled-program basis.

(This resume, if given to a prospective employer, would be one page.)

BETA CORPORATION   1960-1972
Chicago, Illinois
    Divisional Marketing Manager, 1969-72
    Regional Marketing Manager, 1967-69
    National Sales Promotion Manager, 1964-67
    Regional Sales Promotion Manager, 1962-64
    Systems Marketing Manager, 1960-61
Functions and accomplishments include
    .... Originating private trade-show seminars that
produced profitable sales .... a direct-mail program
achieving a 10% return .... a sales training program for
300 men promoting 5,000 items .... reorganizing whole
marketing department to bolster company's position in
marketplace .... personally working with salesmen and
sales managers to produce a 300% increase in sales thru
proper motivation and training .... personally selling
$1,500,000 of equipment while establishing a new market.

CLUB MOTOR COMPANY   1959-1960
Chicago, Illinois
    Systems Analyst

1956-59 .... salesman of multiple business forms for two
small manufacturers
Four years .... U.S. Army .... Captain

EDUCATION: BA, Business Administration and Economics, Ohio State
            University, 1952
PERSONAL   Age - 47   Married - two children
DATA: Available to travel or relocate - U.S. or foreign

all out." Don't say too much. I have told hundreds of clients not to put "Health—Excellent" in a resume. I used to ask them if they had ever seen one that said "Health—Poor." I stopped that line when one of them showed me his resume stating he was subject to epileptic seizures. I could not cure his epilepsy, but I did cure his to-a-fault honesty and his lack of a job.

Under personal you should usually put your age. Your date of birth is a piece of data your next employer doesn't need till it's time to apply for group insurance.

I said you should *usually* show your age on your resume. Never be afraid of being too young. Youth has more energy (it says here!) and more time to grow and learn, and is expected to be able to work harder and longer. Play that up in the resume, the sales letter, and the interviews.

The older person approaches the subject of age differently. You will or will not put age on your resume, based on different factors. If you are looking for a senior position, a consultancy, or a sit-long, do-nothing job, such as a security guard, your age can help sell you in the first two instances. It should not be a hindrance in the last. Rudolf H. was sixty-three and an alien (legal) drawing a pension from the German government when he walked into my office. Today he is sixty-four and still an alien and a pensioner, but he earns twenty dollars an hour as a consultant on foreign taxes to a multinational company. He usually works thirty to forty hours a week.

Personal in the resume can also include professional and business memberships, such as the American Medical Association, professional organizations, and trade associations. If you have held elective or appointive positions, run seminars, or written pamphlets for these organizations, say so.

Personally, I like Mr. Sweet's resume. After all, I wrote it. If you show it to 100 people, such as executive searchers, personnel or human resource managers, career consultants, outplacement specialists, or just good business executives, you will probably get 100 different opinions of what is wrong with it or how it could be improved. In fact, when I look at it a year from now, I'm sure I'll see changes to make. That only means there is no one right way to write a resume.

People who hire or interview others will almost unanimously say Sweet's resume doesn't say enough. I know it doesn't say *too much*.

Although my clients are taught to avoid using their resumes whenever possible, they still have had to use them. And this style of resume has proved successful. Perhaps by not showing all the nice things, it acts like a striptease, causing the recipient to call in the applicant to see (learn) more.

What Is a *Good* Resume?

While I do like Sweet's resume, as well as the others shown (see figures 17, 18, and 19), I do not classify them as *good* ones. A good resume cannot be written unless the requirements of the particular job are known. The applicant should also have good background information on the company and the person who will make the hiring decision. That is why every resume should be tailor-made for each company whenever possible.

I have been lucky enough to be in a position that enabled me to write *good* resumes for five clients. They all resulted in interviews and offers. In fact, one of those clients received three offers for the same job with the same organization. When he turned down the first offer, they raised the price. Later, in a last-ditch effort to hire him, they changed the city to which he would have to relocate. I had helped the company determine the job specifications, most of which were built around my client's background. Obviously, I could do nothing but write a *good* resume in this instance. It was almost entirely different from the original resume I had done for him.

Another one of my *good* resumes helped a man into the number-two position in a corporation listed on the New York Stock Exchange. He's slated to be number one before this book is published. An executive searcher and two psychologists were involved. The psychologists did not like the two-page resume I had prepared. They wanted a twenty pager! I doubt I could write twenty pages about myself, much less a client. He and I outlined the resume together, decided which parts each of us would write, and then wove it all into one sixteen-page resume. I felt a man of his stature should hold his head high and not bow completely to the psychologists by providing twenty pages. The morning it was received, the first psychologist phoned my client to say it was a "masterpiece." That afternoon his partner phoned to congratulate my client on the best resume he had ever seen! Although I must classify it as a good one because it was customized for the need and did get him the job, I still feel it was ridiculous—sixteen pages!

Remember, one page is best, two pages are OK, and three pages might be OK in certain circumstances. Any resume more than three pages won't get the attention you want unless it is perfectly aimed at the job, the company, and the person who can make the offer.

Figures 20, 21, and 22 are functional resumes. A functional resume can be used if you don't want to show too many companies or really want to hide your present employment.

If you are high up in the corporate structure, you should consider answering some resume requests with a letter, rather than a resume, outlining your background. Note Edward Carroll's letter, figure 23. If an inquiry came from a retailer of sporting goods, Ed could easily shorten those paragraphs relating to other products and have room to put his self-selling emphasis on his sporting-goods experience. Likewise, a retailer of sewing machines would get a letter from Ed slanted to that item.

Also remember to get help—a professional or an able friend—if you don't feel satisfied with the resume you wrote.

Your sales letter, ad answers, or other personal marketing approaches still to be presented will produce positive replies. Since most of the positives usually come from the sales letter mailings, we shall discuss how to handle them in the next chapter before becoming involved in other marketing techniques.

Fig. 17   A Resume That Advertises

JUDY SMITH

   3225 Central Ave. . Washington, D.C. 20031 . (202) 555-3607

A D V E R T I S I N G

      P U B L I C   R E L A T I O N S

            C U S T O M E R   R E L A T I O N S

A practical approach to selling products or services through
advertising and public and customer relations. Experienced with
advertising agency and multinational corporation. As an account
executive for an ad agency, provided advertising and PR services
to following industries:

                                  Manufacturers of:

-- Bank   -- Food
-- Brewery   -- Cabinets
-- Insurance carrier   -- Pesticides
-- Residential developer   -- Detergents
-- Professional organization   -- Electric motors

Able researcher, writer, recruiter, trainer ... developer of
promotional plans to increase sales and satisfy customers.

BUSINESS HISTORY:

        TRANSCONTINENTAL VAN LINES, INC.   1971-Present
        Subsidiary of Allied Enterprises
        Washington, D.C.
            Manager of Advertising, PR, and Publications
        Responsible for all above functions, including market
        and customer research; advice to, and direction of,
        outside ad agency and house ad agency; editor-publisher
        of corporate magazine; preparation of films, speeches,
        agent and corporate sales and advertising materials,
        cooperative advertising programs ... establishing the
        corporate image.

(This resume, if given to a prospective employer, would be two pages. The second page should begin
where indicated.)

ADVERTISING, INC.   <u>1969-1970</u>
Portland, Oregon
     <u>Account Executive</u>
For (at that time) Oregon's largest advertising agency,
handled client contract, copy, purchasing. Primary
achievements: created a profitable PR operation plus
planned and prepared all clients' sales aids.

JUDY SMITH   *PAGE TWO*

DANVILLE JUNIOR COLLEGE   <u>1967-1969</u>
Danville, Illinois

PR, English, and Journalism instructor; founder and
adviser of the campus newspaper.

THE BANGKOK POST   <u>1963-1966</u>
Bangkok, Thailand
     <u>Society editor, reporter</u>

THAMMSAT UNIVERSITY   <u>1962-1963</u>
and THAI TECHNICAL INSTITUTE
Bangkok, Thailand

English instructor to Thai students.

THE LOCAL NEWS   <u>1956-1962</u>
Veedersburg, Indiana

Intermittent employment as columnist, advertising and
circulation representative.

<u>EDUCATION</u>:
     MA, English, Indiana University (full scholarship), 1956
     AB, English, Indiana University (full scholarship), 1955
     <u>Wall Street Journal</u> summer scholarship in Journalism at
          University of Texas
     Some work for PhD

PERSONAL DATA:

Age 46
Available to travel and relocate   Single

        Member:
            International Association of Business Communicators
            Advertising Club (AAA affiliate)
            (Winner of top awards from both of above)
            United Way (Chairwoman, Business/Agency Development
                Committee)

Fig. 18 A Resume That Shows a Woman Executive's Qualifications

JANE OLSON

910 North Gulch Blvd.
Spokane, Washington 99201 _____ (509) 555-6080

A D.M I N I S T R A T I V E   E X E C U T I V E

Almost 20 years (many with complete P & L responsibility) managing
hotel/motel operations. Successful in controlling food and
beverage, housekeeping, maintenance, sales--total administration
of all functions necessary to keep guests happy and still earn
profits.

Intelligent, hardworking individual qualified to start up operations
of new hotel/motel properties, supervise daily operations of such
properties, administrate the food and beverage or housekeeping
services of hospitals, health-care facilities, airlines, ship lines,
railroads, clubs, restaurants, or any organization providing food or
lodging.

CAREER . . .

THE BARHAM MOTOR INN   1956-Present
Spokane, Washington
                        Comanager-Part Owner
Built this property from 35 to 105 units. Added meeting rooms.
Established 24-hour service to obtain a railroad housing and
feeding contract, thus attaining a 103% occupancy rate. At various
times responsible for employee management, guests, suppliers and
purchasing, advertising, accounting, setting prices, planning,
financing--overall P & L responsibility. No loss years. Increased
sales every year.

Prior service as cook, waitress, dining-room hostess, desk clerk,
hotel cashier, dining-room manager, comanager of a hotel--and raised
two children.

(This resume, if given to a prospective employer, would be one page.)

EDUCATION . . .

BA, University of Minnesota, 1950. (Earned 100% of college
      education.)

PERSONAL DATA . . .

Age 48 . . . Divorced, two children . . . Will travel, relocate
Active in civic groups   Licensed pilot

Fig. 19   A Resume That Accounts for Years Away from the Business World

ROSEMARY MANN

1233 South 3rd St. ... Williamsville, NY 14221 ... (716) 555-5287

A D M I N I S T R A T O R - - M A N A G E R

Successful manager experienced in customer/client/employee
communication and motivation. A developer of efficient systems and
procedures. Can and has created completely new departments. A
problem solver and troubleshooter who thrives on challenge and
pressure. High intelligence. Good abstract and concrete reasoning.
Maintains knowledge of "pulse" of daily corporate operations.

BUSINESS HISTORY . . .

    JOHN MCKINLEY LIFE INSURANCE CO.   1973-Present
    Williamsville, New York
        Manager, Brokerage Administration, 1974-Present
        Administration Coordinator, 1973-74
        Executive Secretary, 1973
Manages department controlling all matters pertinent to
brokerage operations--provides prompt service to field
personnel. Interfaces with all corporate department heads
and staffs plus field personnel. Responsibilities include
travel to field offices, personal contacts with brokers
and clients, operational analyses, overall promotion of
corporate image. Reports to Chief Operating Officer.

    PHYSICIANS' CLINICAL LABORATORY   January-June 1973
    Buffalo, Michigan
        Supervisor, Office Services
Personnel and office management. Hired and trained personnel,
updated employee manual, developed wage scales, managed all
office procedures.

(This resume, if given to a prospective employer, would be two pages. The second page should begin
where indicated.)

UNIVERSITY OF MICHIGAN   1964-1967
Department of Human Genetics
Ann Arbor, Michigan
     Office Manager, 1965-67
     Departmental Secretary, 1964-65
As above. Instituted careful hiring and training practices
that greatly reduced turnover. Computerized one procedure,
cutting preparation time 75%.

STANDARD MUTUAL LIFE INSURANCE CO.   1958-1959
Boston, Massachusetts
     Secretary to Legal Counsel

NOTE: During missing years, held various positions with fund
raiser, railroad, manufacturer, publisher, and secretarial
service. Primarily wife and mother of two (presently) teenage
sons.

ROSEMARY MANN   *PAGE TWO*

EDUCATION   . . .

     Bachelor of Music/Music History, University of Massachusetts,
        1970
     Management Development Seminars at University of
        Massachusetts:
            Managing the Departmental Office
            Management Communications
            Women in Management
            Orientation to Supervisory Practices
            University Business Procedures

PERSONAL DATA . . .

     Age 40   Married, two children
     Can travel and relocate

Fig. 20   A Functional Chronological Resume

DANIEL D. CALHOUN

265 South Drive   Pekin, Illinois 61554   (309) 555-7186

P R O D U C T / M A R K E T I N G   M A N A G E M E N T

C O N S U M E R   G O O D S

MARKETING EXPERIENCE . . . .

          -- Market-Penetration Analyses
                    Manufacturing Cost Analyses
                    Marketing Results Analyses
          -- Long-Range Product-Line Planning
                    Short-Range Product-Line Planning
          -- New-Product Development
                    Product-Design Development
                    Product-Line Review
                    Product Pricing for Profits
          -- Resource Selection and Evaluation
                    Development of New Suppliers
          -- Accounting Profitability Studies

SALES EXPERIENCE . . . .

          -- Planning for Sales Meetings
                    Training Salesmen
                    Motivating Salesmen
          -- Liquidation of Overstocks
          -- As Assistant Sales Manager, boosted sales on
                    $35,000,000+ product lines

BUSINESS HISTORY . . . .

          -- A MAJOR RETAIL/MAIL ORDER CHAIN   1969-Present
             Chicago, Illinois
                    Associate Buyer, $20,000,000+ lines,
                             1971-Present
                    Assistant National Retail Sales Manager,
                             $35,000,000+ lines, 1971
                    Assistant Buyer, $10,000,000+ lines, 1969-70
                    Trainee, 1969

(This resume, if given to a prospective employer, would be one page.)

```
EDUCATION . . . .

        -- MBA, Marketing, University of Chicago, 1969
        -- BA, Psychology, University of Illinois, 1967

PERSONAL DATA . . . .

        -- Age 27 . . . . . . Married . . . . . .
           Expecting!
```

(Note: Resume didn't mention height and weight. Client was short and fat—we advised a diet!)

Fig. 21   A Consultant's Functional Resume

EARL R. KING
1239 Montclair Avenue
Pittsburgh, Pennsylvania 15237
(412) 555-2716

E N G I N E E R I N G   C O N S U L T A N T

A I R   P O L L U T I O N   C O N T R O L S

Expertise in the application of all types of air pollution control
equipment for industry.
-- Mechanical dust collectors   -- Scrubbers
-- Electrostatic precipitators   -- Fabric collectors
-- Electronic air cleaning   -- Adjustable-speed fluid drives
          -- Metal mill motor room ventilating systems

Equally successful experience with related equipment, including
   -- Ventilating and mechanical draft fans
      -- Air-handling heating and cooling units
         -- Centrifugal compressors
            -- Surface dehumidifiers
               -- Air blenders
                  -- Air washers
                     -- Heat exchangers

Producer of film, writer of articles and guidelines, trainer of
salesmen, seminar leader, speaker ... all on air pollution and
industrial ventilation.

B U S I N E S S   H I S T O R Y

AMERICAN STANDARD, INC.   1963-Present
Industrial Products Division
   -- Branch Manager, 1971-Present
   -- Manager, Industrial Systems, Air Pollution Control Dept., 1970
   -- Air Pollution Control Specialist, 1968-70
   -- Branch Manager (Sales), 1963-68

WESTINGHOUSE ELECTRIC CORP.   1954-1963
Sturtevant Division
   -- Sales Engineer, Air-Handling Apparatus

(This resume, if given to a prospective employer, would be one page.)

<u>E D U C A T I O N</u>

BS, Mechanical Engineering, University of Pittsburgh, 1952
Specialized courses:
    Industrial Air Pollution Control, University of Michigan, 1969
    Business and Management Program, University of Pittsburgh,
      1956-58
Plus several technical courses on air handling, heating and
    ventilating, air conditioning, and electronic air cleaning
U. S. Army Work Simplification Course

<u>P E R S O N A L   D A T A</u>

Age 49 . . . . . Will travel and relocate . . . . . Married, 2 children
Memberships: Air Pollution Control Association
               Association of Iron and Steel Engineers

Fig. 22   An Air Force Officer's Functional Resume

PAUL GREEN

1605 E. Wells Street * Colorado Springs, Colorado 80951 * (303)555-8513

C O M M U N I C A T I O N S   C O N S U L T A N T

Unusually broad experience administering specialized radio, teletype, and telephone communications serving customers around the world. Technical background in all types of communications equipment.

Highlights of administrative responsibilities

- Administrative Director, Telecommunications Division, U.S.A.F., Okinawa

- Base Communications & Electronics Officer, Chambley Air Base, France

- Director of Language Laboratory, U.S.A.F. Academy

- Budget Administrator, Department of Foreign Languages, U.S.A.F. Academy

- Builder of three civilian apartment buildings and a $1,500,000 air force installation

Face-to-face communications history includes

- Course Director, Associate Professor of German, U.S.A.F. Academy

- Lecturer, Business Administration, University of Maryland

- Assistant Professor, World Political Geography, University of Akron

- Coordinator of international functions, U.S.A.F.

- Briefing officials of cabinet and senatorial rank plus foreign dignitaries

- International protocol activities

(This resume, if given to a prospective employer, would be one page.)

EDUCATION   . . .

Completed all but dissertation for PhD in Institutional
  Management and Business Administration, University of Denver
MBA, Industrial Management, University of Akron, 1962
BS, Education, University of Akron, 1960
BA, Economics & Political Science, Mercer University, 1951
  Law school, two years
TV and electronic courses at American Television Laboratories
  and Illinois Institute of Technology
Over 12 U.S.A.F. courses in communications, human relations,
  counseling, teaching, and management
(Author of three-volume textbook and laboratory manual on
  German language currently used by several institutions of
  higher education)

PERSONAL DATA . . .

Age 50 . . . Married . . . Available to relocate and/or
travel anywhere . . . Fluent in German . . . Fair in French
. . . Passing in Hungarian . . . Highest security clearances

Fig. 23

EDWARD S. CARROLL
10 South Lake Road
Kenilworth, Illinois   60043
(312) 555-8380

Date

Name, Title
Company
Street Address
City, State, Zip Code

Dear _____:

You ask about my business history. It is 100% XYZ Retailers, with
a variety of products--hard and soft lines, big and small tickets.

This began in 1949 as a part-time salesclerk in Ithaca, New York.
The only years away from XYZ were while in the infantry.

In 1952 I received my first managerial assignment as Division Manager of Catalog Sales. My product-line background was broadened
with positions as Division Manager of Women's Clothing, Housewares,
Sporting Goods, and Automotive.

Then, as Group Merchandise Manager of three Buffalo stores, I had
20 division managers representing over 55 product lines reporting
to me.

In 1963, I was promoted to HQs as Assistant National Retail Sales
Manager-Housewares. Later, over a five-year span in Sporting
Goods, I earned four promotions (including National Retail Sales
Manager) up to Senior Buyer.

Following a staff assignment in the General Merchandise Office as
a Group Buying Coordinator of 12 merchandising departments, I was
made National Merchandise Manager of all home maintenance products,
sewing machines, cabinets, and sewing accessories.

After two years in the above position, I returned to the Sporting
Goods Department (XYZ's second largest department) as National
Manager. My management and marketing successes resulted in my promotion to Sporting Goods Group National Merchandising Manager with
sales over $500 million.

Personal data: age 44, married, three children, active in civic
affairs.

Sincerely,

Edward S. Carroll

6

Handling Your
Positive Replies

Now you are getting letters or phone calls as a result of sending out sales letters, answering ads, and using personal contacts and other sales approaches discussed in this book. What do you do with them besides patting yourself on the back? You pat yourself on the back orally to your respondents! You will also, and this is very important, pat them on the back, too.

Phone Your Positives

Every positive response deserves a phone call from you as soon as possible after its receipt. Your card file of companies to whom you sent your sales letter should be kept by your telephone. Then, if a company phones you instead of replying by letter, you can readily look it up to reidentify its size, products, etc. You are always ready to talk, whether the company calls or you call.

To learn what to say, let us first learn what the company will write to you if there is an interest in interviewing you. The letter will pleasantly and efficiently request additional information, such as a resume, college transcript, or salary history. In a very few instances you might receive a letter asking you to call for an interview appointment, with no other questions asked.

No matter how pleasant the letter is that asks for additional information, you should realize it is actually saying:

Dear _____:

We have your letter. You sound good to us. But, before we spend any of our time or money interviewing you, we need to know more. Please provide us with. . . . If we are still interested, we'll contact you again.

The Jones Company

It is not unusual to get a letter stating there are no openings now that fit your qualifications but asking you to send a resume or answer specific questions so that a file can be started on you in case of future needs. Such a letter certainly does not sound like a positive reply, but you should classify it as such because it *might* really be one. Maybe the company is writing to you in this way because it is afraid of the reaction of a present employee who did see or can see this correspondence. Or, it may feel you have a particular interest in joining its ranks, and it doesn't want you to get too excited over that prospect in advance. After all, your sales letter, being personalized, should give the impression that you wrote only to them or a few selected firms.

So, a positive response is *any* request for additional information, and you should handle all positives with a phone call to the person who replied to you. Hopefully, it will be the executive (your potential boss) to whom you wrote. Express your excitement over the request for more facts about you. Say you are happy because you know so many good things about the company, such as the reputation of its products, its standing in the industry—anything that pats the person on the back and also shows you truly know the company.

Fill Out Any Application Before Phoning

If the letter enclosed an application for you to fill out, do so before phoning (see chapter 8) and say you have it in your hand. Ask that you be allowed to deliver it because you want the person to meet

you. Don't expect compliance with this request. The person is going to want to see your application first. You phoned only to show that you are way above the level of all the other job seekers, and that you also know the company and have an idea of how you would fit into it. Out of every 1,000 applications mailed, I'll bet only one applicant makes the investment of a phone call to convey particular interest in the company.

You filled out the application before phoning so that it could be mailed immediately after the call. As I keep repeating, do not send it with a cover letter. Send it with another *sales*-type letter. This letter should remind the person of your phone call, say something nice about the company, sell yourself as the one who can do the job, and ask for an interview.

Always Phone Positives from Ad Answers

This phone-call system works extremely well for positive replies to your ad answers and best for positives from blind ads. Run, do not walk, to the library to look up every company that sends a positive response to a blind ad. Then you can phone to say, "I was thrilled to learn Box 399 is the RST Company. I've known and respected RST for years. In fact, I use RST myself." Or words to that effect.

These phone calls will give you a real edge over your competition. Try them.

Phone Those Who Request Resumes

If a positive reply requests a resume, phone and, after saying something nice about the company and your abilities, ask for an interview. If the person requests a resume first, say you know that resumes are usually used to weed people out, primarily because sometimes the qualifications most pertinent to a particular job have been left out of a resume, since nobody's entire background and qualifications can be put on a few pages. Say you'd very much appreciate an interview— that if necessary, you will bring the resume along. Again, as in the request for an application, you will probably have to send the resume first to get the interview. But do send it with a sales-type letter, as for an application.

Don't Allow Yourself to Be Interviewed on the Phone

Try your best not to be interviewed over the phone. You already know you are far better off not talking salary before an interview. Try to avoid salary or other questions on the phone by saying this matter is far too important to you to handle any other way than face-to-face. After all, your possible career with the company is at stake. In chapter 16 on negotiating, you will learn some ways to avoid such salary discussion. Right now just realize you must try not to talk salary on the phone, but not to the extent that you make an enemy or lose any chance for the interview.

Also, because you are now seeking an interview as the result of a positive reply to your original contact (usually a sales letter), do not try to find out what the interviewers have in mind for you. While it would be marvelous to know this, your aim is to get into the interview face to face, preferably in their offices.

In these phone calls or in the positive reply, you may be asked how you came to write to that particular company. Your answer should be either that you knew of the great attributes of the company (name some) or that you did research to select the best companies in that industry.

Tape-record These Phone Calls

It would be a wise move to tape-record these phone calls. You won't need to take any notes, as you'll have it all on tape. This will enable you to talk much easier. Also, you can critique and improve your phone handling by playing back the tapes. Call the least interesting companies first. Practice on them. Make mental or written notes on how you can improve before phoning the prospects that are most important to you.

I'll never forget the reactions of a client with a Ph.D. in film, radio, and TV. For some reason these phone calls terrified him! He could make tapes of himself doing his regular job but not while he was selling himself. I had to listen to his tapes and advise him on how to improve his phone technique. It obviously worked for one of his calls, since he received an offer from Muzak.

It is easy to tape a phone conversation with a cassette recorder. You will need a telephone attachment sold by most radio or electronic stores. These are small induction coils usually held to the telephone receiver by a simple rubber suction cup. They can cost as little as one dollar and are plugged directly into your recorder. You should take the recorder to the store to make sure you are getting a compatible attachment.

Remember, your phone calls to positive responses are aimed at selling yourself to the prospective employers. This does not mean you will make appointments for interviews with these calls. You have sold yourself as having something special on the ball. You will be remembered for that.

Expect the Company to Pay Interview Expenses

Most of your interviews will be arranged in later phone calls. If the interview is out of town, it is customary for the company to pay your expenses. Let them know you expect them to pay for the trip. Do not ask whether they will. That shows weakness on your part and may result in a negative reply. Instead, ask how they want the travel reservations handled.

It is not advisable to go out of town for an interview if the company refuses to cover the costs. Two clients of mine have done this over my strong objections. Both got what I considered to be low offers from the companies and, again over my objections, accepted the offers. Both phoned me within a few months to tell me how unhappy they were with their new cheap employers. Then I had the problem of overcoming my urge to say "I told you so."

Follow Up Your Positives

Follow up every positive approximately three weeks after your last action if you have not heard anything in those three weeks. Phone those who seemed to appreciate your initial phone calls. Write those who did not. In either case, try again to sell yourself into an interview. Say you sent the application, the resume, or whatever on such and such a date. You are checking to make sure it was received and to find out what additional information might be needed. Further, you want to make sure you are still being considered.

Again, avoid Mondays. Don't phone those positives on a Monday, and do not mail a letter to arrive on a Monday.

Figure 24 is a Lead Report Form to be used to record your positives and to keep a running score on your results. The Source column tells you which approach generated each positive. You will find sales letter recorded most often here. Under Action Taken show you phoned, sent a resume or an application, arranged an interview, etc. Be sure to record the dates of each action to remind yourself when follow-up action is indicated.

Later, since some positives will turn into negatives, you may want to use figure 25 to relist the positives still open. Keep all your correspondence and notes regarding each company clipped or stapled together, with the most current paper on top. Keep them in alphabetical order by the telephone in case a positive should phone you after receipt of your resume, application, or other paperwork you sent.

Don't overlook the negative replies you will receive in response to the sales letter. Read the next chapter.

Fig. 24

L E A D   R E P O R T   F O R M

Week Ending _____ 19 _____

No. Positives Received This Week _____ To Date _____

No. Negatives Received This Week _____ To Date _____

LIST ALL POSITIVES BELOW

Source	Company & Individual	Action Taken

Fig. 25

POSITIVES STILL OPEN

No.	Source	Company & City	If Inter-viewed	Status
1				
2				
3				
4				
5				
6				
7				
8				
9				
10				

7

How and Why
You Reply
to Some Negatives

Don't be discouraged by the flood of negatives you will receive in reply to your sales letter. Be very unhappy if you get only a few negative responses. A lack of such replies means your letter was so poor or unappealing that nobody thought it worth the trouble to answer you.

No matter how good your sales letter is, a majority of the recipients will not bother to answer it. They don't know you. You sent them an unsolicited letter, and they have no need for your particular services at the time. So they threw it away!

Most of the replies you will receive will be negatives—not positives previously defined as a request for more information. Over the years I have found that negatives are either useless form letters or honest statements of regret over the inability of the company to use a good person now or in the foreseeable future. The form letters almost always come from personnel departments, who may or may not have taken the trouble to read the sales letter.

What Happens to Letters to Company Presidents

Letters to presidents of the larger companies are rarely seen by the presidents. Instead, they are almost automatically sent to personnel.

That is why I encouraged you to send your letters to the executive who would most likely be your boss if you are hired.

If Gerald Ford were to mail a sales letter to the presidents of Fortune 500 companies, I'll bet he would get many negative form letters from many personnel departments. After all, the negatives go out automatically in too many instances. They would not realize they were writing to a former president.

Once I sent a sales letter over my signature to thirty-one corporate presidents telling each of them a man he knew personally in an executive position in his industry was looking to make a change. After describing the man's abilities to fit into the president's organization, I concluded by offering to arrange a meeting if the president was interested. Among the replies were sixteen form letters from personnel people saying although *my* qualifications were excellent they had *no need for me.*

But, the individually dictated negatives are very important to you. They are proof the letter was read. They may give you some idea of strengths to push further in another sales letter or in interviews. I have seen sales letters so good that the negative replies stated not only sincere regrets but also offered job-search advice or introductions to other companies.

Catalog Your Negative Replies—Write to Some with a Resume

At any rate, you should save all your negative replies. Set up a cross-reference file system of your mailing-list cards and negative replies. The cards should be filed by geographical area, and the letters alphabetically. Why? Because you are going to call on some of those respondents when and if possible. You are also going to write to everyone who was *honestly* complimentary to you about your letter or your background.

Your written reply to such negatives should obviously thank them for writing. Remind them you are particularly interested in the company, tell them more about what you can do, and enclose your resume or a specially written resume aimed at them. Your sales letter did not include a resume. They may find something in your resume now that will attract them, primarily because you are showing initiative by responding to their negative.

Call on Some Negatives

Let's discuss calling on some negative replies. Such calls produce interviews or referrals. You filed your mailing-list cards geographically and cross-referenced them with the negatives so that you would know whom to call on whenever you happened to get into a particular neighborhood or city. Suppose you are going to Atlanta for an interview, on business for your present employer, for a vacation, or for any reason. Save time to call on the person who sent you the negative. Just walk in without an appointment. Tell the receptionist you are from out of town (name your home city) and that you and Mr. Smith (the man who replied to you) have had correspondence. You should be able to get in to see him because of those two factors.

When you are in his office, one of you will almost immediately bring up the subject of the *negative* response. So why are you there?

"Because, Mr. Smith, I am enough of a salesperson to believe no sale is actually made unless the buyer first says or thinks no. That's only order writing—not selling. In addition, your letter really said, 'Not now, maybe later.' I feel that by meeting each other, it will be possible to make later an awful lot sooner!'"

If you are looking for a sales-related position, this approach will often result in consideration for a job. The odds are somewhat lower for others. Either way, Mr. Smith will appreciate your aggressiveness and give you an *E* for effort. If he tells you he has no idea when his company could use you, thank him for seeing you and ask what other company or companies you should see in his area or industry.

Get Referrals—Try for Introductions

You want more than company names. If asked for the person to see, Mr. Smith will tell you. Then ask for permission to say he sent you. If he is truly cooperative, you should ask him if he would be kind enough to introduce you over the phone. As stated later in chapter 15 on interviewing, you should assure him you will carry the ball with that company from that point on.

In summary, I should tell you that replies by mail to the *better* negatives produce a handful of offers to my clients each year. Calls on negatives and cold calls produce even more. Calls on negatives are terrific sales tools for sales and marketing people. Cold calls, as discussed in chapter 13, will work for anybody.

8

Make a Company Application Sell for You

Hardly anyone, including executives, seems exempt these days from the need to fill out applications. Most companies request a resume or an application before they will grant an interview, because they are really trying to determine in advance whether interviewing you will be productive for them. If you can't convince them by phone or letter how well you fit their operation, you will have to provide a resume (tailored to their needs, I hope) or fill out an application.

Don't provide both the resume and the application unless they specifically request both. The application tells them what they want to know about you in a format familiar to them. Any selling points you can't put into the application should be easy to include in the personal selling letter you are going to send with the application. Never mail a resume, an application, or any information without a sales-type letter requesting an interview.

Some applications ask you to fill them out in pencil in your own handwriting. Think before you write. Write neatly. The pencil reply is requested to see how many erasures you make—and where. Your personal handwriting may be used to help analyze your character, attitudes, and disposition by a graphologist or somebody else deemed capable of making such determinations. Of course, the company wants to know that you can write legibly and spell accurately.

Some Application "Don'ts"

I personally would refuse to fill out an application in a company's office just prior to a scheduled interview. My excuse would be that the possibility of a position with that "great" firm was too important to allow me to fill it out in a hurry. Any time spent on the application could more profitably be spent with the proper people in the company. Offer to prepare the application at home after the interview. Or, if necessary, suggest you come back another time for the interview.

Many applications ask for expected starting salary or minimum salary requirements. Leave it blank, explaining in the letter that the chance to join such a good company is more important than salary to you. In a way, you'll be showing your expectations anyway with your salary history.

Use Your Resume in Filling Out Applications

Every application will request business history. Be sure to use your resume as a guide. This means you should list only those positions and dates (years) that appear in your resume. You will be asked to put down why you left each job. Your answers should always relate to an improvement in your career. More salary, growth industry, better position, and the opportunity to broaden your capabilities are accepted and understood reasons.

Do give the names of your superiors, but make it clear, either on the application or in the letter, that your present employer must not be contacted as it will jeopardize your present situation.

Give Salary History on Applications

Although you should not divulge salary history on your resume or in an ad answer or your sales letter, you will have to give it on an application. If you don't, the odds are you won't get the interview. This is another reason for phoning all positives and trying to presell yourself.

Censor These . . .

While you must answer the salary-history question to get the interview, you should not answer any other dollar questions on an application. For example, How much other income do you have? What is your spouse's income? The cost or market value of your home? Monthly mortgage or rental?

The company wants to know how hungry you are so that it can control the interview and the negotiations. I've been advising clients for years to leave those portions blank. That action may have cost a few interviews, but I'll bet those clients ended up in better jobs with companies better than the firms who held out for all the answers. I do know my clients got positions where these questions were asked but not answered.

If the application asks for references, give as many as requested. But, be sure to request on the application or in your letter that references not be checked until after a definite mutual interest has been established in the interview. The use of references is described in chapter 12.

Finally, don't put anything in an application that could possibly make a company not want to hire you. I'm sure you are now telling yourself you would never do such a thing. Have you ever shown a geographical preference? That is probably a limiting factor to a company with many locations. You can't be transferred easily. Get the interview without bringing such a matter up. Perhaps the job in Upper Slobovia has so many advantages that you won't want to turn it down.

Do not proudly show on an application your willingness to travel 25, 50, or even 75 percent of the time. I agree that these figures can sound high, but they still show limits. Instead, answer any question regarding time you are willing to spend traveling by saying you will travel as much as is required to get the job done. This will not obligate you to accept a position with too much travel. It will help you get the interview.

Remember to use the application as another selling tool. You are using it to sell yourself into the right job. There are more selling tools still to be discussed. Chapter 9 brings up two that I think are used all too seldom. Yet they produce real results when used according to a plan.

9

Use of Business and Personnel News

When looking for a new position, you must always keep your eyes and ears open for ideas about a company or industry that may possibly have an opening for you. An expanding company needs more people. An organization moving its headquarters a few miles within a city or hundreds of miles to a different city will need new blood because some people will not make the move. This is sometimes true at all levels. Perhaps 5 percent of my clients sought help because they did not want to move with their company even though it offered to do many things to make such a move palatable.

Double Approach

You should be reading the daily papers and trade journals for any information that could produce a job lead. Such leads can also come from news items about personnel changes at high levels. New executives will make changes in the personnel reporting to them. They won't do so immediately but will wait (if they are true executives) until they are more sure of their moves. This delay is good from your standpoint. Since there probably won't be a public announcement for one to three months after an executive has started a new job, you can make your approach at the time when some changes are actually being planned.

If you are lucky enough to know the executive personally, try to arrange a visit at the office. If that's not possible, a phone call can start the ball rolling. If you do not know the person, you should still try to get in the door, phone, or write.

In the case of an executive leaving one firm for another, there might be two companies interested in you. The old company has probably found a replacement by the time you read of the change in the newspaper. But the replacement will be making changes and should be contacted.

It is not difficult to learn the name of the replacement at the old company. Just phone and ask the receptionist for the name and correct title of, for example, the head of the sales department. Explain that you want to send some information and ask how the name is spelled. Don't take spelling for granted—Smith can well be spelled Smythe.

Tailor a Sales Letter to Business News

Howard C. used business news to get a top-notch position in purchasing management. News of expansion or even a new annual report from a corporation gave him enough background to write to chief executive officers and tell them very specifically how his purchasing controls and methods could save them millions each year. Howard usually quoted the company's dollar volume of purchases and the percentage of purchases to total operating costs and profits. Three large organizations not far from home were practically bidding for his services.

One of his letters, edited to prevent company identification, is shown as figure 26. If you give it thought, you can come up with a personalized sales-letter mailing like this. It takes more time and thought than the sales letter described earlier in this book as your number-one technique in job hunting. It is more expensive, since these letters cannot be mass produced; but if done right, it pays off better on a letter-by-letter basis.

Fig. 26

HOWARD C.

12345 S. 6th Street * New York, New York 10004 * (212) 555-3353

Date

John Smythe, President
TMC Corporation
Street Address
City, State, Zip Code

Dear Mr. Smythe:

Increasing costs have been expressed as a concern in your 1977 and
1978 annual reports, and this concern is also mentioned in Barron's
July 3, 1979, review of TMC. With purchased cost of materials and
services probably accounting for over 50% of your MLO (Material,
Labor, and Overhead), it would seem an imperative responsibility for
TMC management to assure that purchasing is performed in a professional manner. Since it is the largest cost element, it offers the
greatest potential for profit improvement, i.e., the leverage
available through reductions in costs of materials and supplies
probably outweighs similar reductions in labor costs by a ratio of
5 or 6 to 1.

In this regard, the two areas where my experience has shown the
greatest potential for lowering purchased costs are improved purchasing performance at Divisional Purchasing Departments and
selectively utilizing the cumulative purchasing volume of those
operations in negotiating regional, national, and international
purchasing agreements. My area of expertise is doing exactly
that--in a large multinational corporation with decentralized,
geographically dispersed profit centers.

With operating revenues projected to exceed $325 million this year,
it would appear TMC can benefit from guidance by a purchasing
professional experienced in working with decentralized, autonomous
profit centers. Specialized purchasing experience is required to
accomplish these cost-reduction objectives without disturbing
divisional autonomy. This is my forte.

May we discuss how I can help improve TMC's profits?

Very truly yours,

Howard C.

10

Selling Yourself
in Psychological Tests

Some companies still require these tests. It is interesting that many want them only when filling or creating openings at senior levels. Others make them a requirement for middle-management positions.

The major point is you will take a psychological test if the company so demands and you want that particular job. You can try to talk your way out of it by reselling your accomplishments and achievements in the business world as evidence that you are OK psychologically. However, you'll probably lose that argument because the importance of the test results to the hiring decision will be verbally played down.

You Can Beat a Psychologist's Adverse Report

I do know of a few instances where the candidate was hired despite an adverse report from the psychologist. Before accepting my client as executive vice-president, a corporate president insisted the client take such a test. The psychologists reported my client and the president were of such different personalities they would never get along together. The president resented such remarks about *his* personality and promptly hired the client!

In a few other cases the candidate either were so badly needed or had so effectively sold themselves they were hired despite heavily qualified psychological reports.

Psychologists Usually Say "If in Doubt, Out"

Sorry to say, I've yet to see a report without qualifications. Of course, this is because nobody is perfect. Also because the psychologists no doubt want to protect themselves. They look bad if a highly recommended applicant is hired and later turns out to be wrong for the job. More than one psychological-testing firm obeys the rule: If in doubt, out.

Enough negatives. Only a small fraction of my clients have had to take such tests to get their jobs, and I can remember only two who were turned down as a result. The odds are in your favor. I'm going to teach you what I taught them on handling this matter.

Six Rules for "Passing" a Psychological Test

There are certain fundamental rules to follow before and during psychological tests. *First,* get a good night's sleep. I can't tell you how to do this other than to exercise moderately so that you will go to bed tired. Do not use sleeping pills or tranquilizers to get that sleep. Their aftereffects during the test can do you more harm than good.

Second, psych yourself into a positive mood. Think, write, and talk only in positives. Don't knock anybody or any firm. Meet both the test and the psychologist as a happy, alert person.

Third, be consistent.

Fourth, come across as the type of person fitting the job specialty for which you are being tested.

Consistency and properly representing yourself can be discussed together. A financial manager is expected to be more of an introvert, a reader, chess player, etc., while the sales manager has more outside, people-related activities. I know many successful financial and sales managers who are just the opposite. But by consistently answering questions and providing self-descriptions that fit the looked-for pattern, you improve your chances.

Fifth, avoid absolutes. If you are asked a question with absolutes, such as *always* or *never*, be careful. Do not list as true rather than false a statement like "I have never stolen anything in my life." What person hasn't stolen small things, especially when a child? These lies can make the psychologist ask deeper questions. Mark as false, "I've never taken more than my fair share of anything."

Sixth, try to answer all questions on written tests. On the untimed tests, there are usually no right or wrong answers. For instance, there may be three statements of possible actions. You are asked which action you would be most likely to take and which least likely. Give the truest answers. Often you would not have taken any of those actions. Remember, your replies are limited to listed possibilities, and among them you will show which you would choose or cast aside. Try to be consistent in your approach.

Timed tests are usually different in that there can be right and wrong answers. If you are weak in math, practice addition, subtraction, multiplication, division, square roots, percentages, and fractions before taking the tests.

How to Cheat a Little

A timed multiple-choice test allows you to cheat a little. Answer every question you can first. Then back up and devote more time to the tougher ones. When the time is up, hurriedly fill in any answers to the remaining unanswered questions. If you are to put your answers into little circles or squares on a timed test with actual right or wrong answers, rest assured they are scored by a template laid over your answer sheet. Guess right and your fill-in will show through the hole. Your score increases. If your guess or fill-in is wrong, in most cases it won't count against you any more than if you had put in no answer to that question.

"In most cases" above refers to the fact that there are some tests for which the scoring formula does penalize guessing. Therefore, read the instructions for each test carefully. If incorrect guessing is penalized, the instructions will tell you. If the instructions make no mention of it, you can safely answer all questions even if you are making wild guesses.

The penalties for guessing wrong are not so big. Typically, you will receive one full credit for every question answered correctly and be penalized only one-fourth credit for every wrong answer.

Don't Show Any Impatience

Don't show any impatience or allow yourself to be impatient. My impatience almost cost me a job once. A psychological test I was taking had, among many other things, four pages of sentences to be completed. On the first three pages, I completed sentences beginning with "My mother" by making positive statements about her. On the fourth page my impatience came out. I wrote "What! Again?" When I met with the psychologist, he started out by telling me I was not the man for the job, as I was too impatient. I actually surprised him by asking whether he was referring to "My mother." We then agreed it was a sense of humor rather than impatience that characterized my reply.

Sentence-Completion Tests

The sentence completions should be positive. For example, "Work is _____" should not be ended with "drudgery." Better, "Work is fun and rewarding." My favorite sentence completion is "When he saw the boss coming, _____." A majority of the replies I have seen refer to the fact that when *he* saw the boss coming, *he* started to work harder. That's bad. The person who writes that is telling the psychologist he works hard only when being watched. After all, *he* is the man (or woman) taking the test. Wouldn't it be better to write something like "When he saw the boss coming, he looked up with a smile"? The implications of a happy, able, hard worker are there.

Draw-a-Picture Tests

Some psychological tests let you forget it is *you* you are writing about. Have you ever been asked to draw a picture of a person? Next you were asked to turn the drawing over and write a short story about that person. Please don't draw a picture of somebody of the opposite sex—or of somebody lying in the sun. There is no telling what conclusions will be reached about you if your picture and story are about the opposite sex. You will be seen as not having much of a desire to work if your drawing and story relate to leisure, sports, a hobby, or even a social event. It is always best to draw somebody on the job, with feet planted firmly on the floor and one hand holding merchandise or papers. Your story relates how this person (with a name other than your own) is doing something destined to bring more sales, cut costs, or just plain boost profits. The psychologist considers what you put on this paper as either how you see yourself or how you would like to see yourself. And—your ability to draw is of no interest at all.

Thematic Apperception Tests

You might be given thematic apperception tests. In these you are presented with several pictures that for the most part seem to portray sad or ambiguous events. You are asked to write a short story brought to mind by each picture. Try to convert them to positive stories with happy endings. Be sure your stories stress achievement, success, and positive relationships rather than conflict.

Self-Description Words

You will also probably be presented with a list of words and told to check those that fit you. Since there are both positive and negative words, you are told to check off a minimum number of negatives. The positives are easy. But don't forget that there are many positives with almost equal meaning in the list. If you check off *responsible*, be sure to check such words as *dependable, trustworthy, conscientious,* and *determined.*

Negatives aren't so easy. The financial person can check off *conventional, inhibited, introverted,* and *reserved.* The general manager or sales/marketing management type could be *suspicious, sensitive, extravagant, egotistical, crafty,* and even *self-centered.* Pick words to check off that can fit your occupation.

If you are asked to come up with words of your own that best describe you, choose words that you would have liked to put in your sales letter and resume or use in an interview. The resume and sales letter should be factual, but in writing them you did think of descriptive adjectives about your personality you would have liked to use.

Your greatest asset to a psychologist is probably a healthy and happy background as a child and a healthy and happy life now as an adult. You are a person who likes to be around people, and others like to be with you. You have a sense of well-being and a sense of humor.

To summarize, it is foolish to worry about taking psychological tests. I have never recommended any reading material to prepare for them, as it is more important to be as much like yourself as possible, modified only by the six fundamental rules presented in this chapter. If a test is in your future, reread this chapter and relax yourself into a positive mood. *Frankly, if the company wants you enough, it will hire you despite the opinions of a psychologist.*

11

Using Your
Interview Kit

An interview kit consists of documentation proving you have held certain positions and providing evidence of some of your accomplishments. Properly used, it will close the credibility gap existent in almost all interviews. If you use it during interviews in a way that does not bore the interviewers, they will begin to believe everything you tell them. Please do not misunderstand me. I am not telling you to lie. I am merely stating that newspaper and magazine articles of late do advise lying, and many interviewers therefore expect it. They will appreciate you if you are prepared to prove your statements.

In the Interview Kit

Exactly what should you put in your kit? To begin with, understand it should not be so thick or stuffed that the interviewers want to hide from it. It can contain such items as reports of your promotions; letters of commendation; examples of your writings, whether a manual, a memo, or a newspaper article; pictures of assembly lines, products, or manufacturing plants with which you have been involved; photocopies of large purchase orders resulting from your efforts; or anything that fits your particular work background and the position you are seeking.

Not in the Interview Kit

Your interview kit should *not* contain pictures of your spouse, children, or home, your pets, or your hobbies unless they are very closely related to the job; and it should *not* include your resume or the reference list described in the next chapter.

You should not bring a resume to an interview, since you want the interviewer to listen to you—not use the resume as a crutch to ask you questions. Of course, if you are asked in advance to bring it, you should. But do not offer it. Keep it in your pocket until asked for it. With luck and ability on your part, the matter might be forgotten.

How to Use It

The actual use of the interview kit is an art, not a science. Take care not to bore the interviewers. All you want them to do is to glance quickly at it one or two times. That is usually enough to make them believe what you say.

To make it easy for them to take quick glances and for you to find what you want to show, it is best to put all single or unbound sheets in a loose-leaf binder. Put dividers in it so you can easily locate and turn to any particular item in a hurry. Let it remain in your briefcase on the floor next to your chair. When you start discussing a subject contained in your kit, pull it out of your briefcase and lay it on the desk open to the page you want to show. Aim the binder at the right hand of the interviewers (unless they're left-handed), point to the page or a particular item on the page, and tell a bit about it. They will glance at the page but will probably not read it. You aim the binder at their hand instead of their eyes to entice them to pick it up.

Tell about your "exhibit" in only two or three sentences, whether or not it receives more than a casual glance. The very fact that you have written documentation proves your point.

Let the binder lie on the desk. Later in the interview you may come to another matter contained in your kit. If so, just reach over and turn to the proper page, call attention to it, and again limit yourself to a few sentences about it.

Be sure to pick up your interview kit at the end of the session— unless you are asked to leave it behind. In that case, be sure you know when and how you are to get it back.

Censoring Company Proprietary Information

Obviously, your kit must be censored to eliminate any information your present or past employers would not like made available to outsiders. It can easily be censored with scissors or by blacking out certain items, such as customer names or dollar volumes. Your prospective employer will score up another plus for you for protecting others.

Emphasizing Your Accomplishments

The opposite of censoring is highlighting, which should be done to call immediate attention to your part in the actions shown. Highlighters are available. They are broad-based felt-tip pens containing a yellow transparent ink. When used over your name or certain sentences, this ink will make them leap out at the reader.

Everybody Should Have One

It is my suggestion that you start now building up an interview kit even if you are not yet actively in the job market. Everybody should be saving such material, starting with his or her very first job. It might not be used in a job-search campaign, but just reading about your own successes will certainly help you hold your head higher both on and off the present job. This is further discussed as a "hero file" in chapter 18.

12

Make References
Work for You

Your references can be extremely important—or of no consequence.
They are important if your prospective employer checks them. They
are of no consequence if your references are never contacted by
companies interested in you. Believe it or not, most companies do *not*
check references! To go a step further, I have found that most companies that ask for them do not follow up with reference checks.
Over the years I have had several clients offered positions subject to
a check yet to be made on references. Although most of those reference checks were not made, the clients are now solidly entrenched in
their new jobs.

In the week prior to my writing this chapter, four clients accepted
new positions. Because this subject was on my mind, I asked them, as
we evaluated their offers, whether their references had been
checked. All four told me the new employers had not even asked for
references.

About three weeks ago another client accepted the number-two
position in a corporate division. He was told his then present employer would be called to verify salary history, titles, and years of

employment. My client resigned his old job effective the next week. Based on a phone call to him today, I can relate that the new employer has not made the check. I bet he never will.

Why References Are Not Always Checked

Many companies these days do not go through the formality of checking references, since they realize it is only a formality. Your former employers are limited as to what they can say about you by various legal constraints. They are also afraid of letting their emotions show up in their descriptions of you! In fact, many large companies have a policy whereby reference requests are handled only by the personnel department, and answers are confined to dates of employment and jobs or titles held.

Who Should Be on Your Reference List

Since your references might be checked, you must consider them an important part of your job-search campaign. Be assured that a good executive recruiter will check them. Your reference list should be business related and have few if any relatives or friends on it. If possible, it should contain superiors, peers, and subordinates. To maintain the security of your present job, it is probably wise not to include your boss on the list. Perhaps you can comfortably and safely talk with other people in the company and enlist their cooperation and confidentiality.

Test Your References in Advance

Then you should have a friend contact each person to see how these people will handle questions about you. Your friend can call them individually or send a letter on company stationery to make it look as if you were being considered for a position.

We ask our clients for names and addresses of ten or more people who know their business capabilities. They are warned not to list their present employer or anyone who might possibly tell him of this reference check. It is suggested they add any prominent people whose endorsements could be of benefit. Our clients are asked not to inform anybody in advance, with the possible exception of those individuals in the company who should be approached first to maintain confidentiality.

Then we send these people a letter something like this:

Dear Mr. Smith:

We are interested in Nancy B. Jones as a candidate for an important financial management position. Any information you can give us as to her management qualifications, financial and accounting abilities, and overall personality will be helpful to us.

Thank you.

This letter does not go out on our regular letterhead showing us as personal marketing and outplacement consultants. Instead, we use a letterhead identifying our company as executive consultants. We don't want the recipients to know we are helping Nancy Jones find a new job.

You will note our reference request does not ask a list of specific questions. It tells very little about the job Nancy Jones is to fill. By not confining the reference's reply, we enable him to tell us more of what he really thinks about Jones. The answers to our letter tell us whom to use as references and whom never to use.

Handling Adverse References

Occasionally we receive a reply from an individual that is 95 percent good and 5 percent bad. That 5 percent, if it covers a vital matter, could cost Jones a job. We ask Jones to bring up the negative in person or by phone to try for an assurance that it won't be repeated on other reference requests. If no such assurance is forthcoming, that person is obviously not going to be used as a reference.

Some negative information or replies as part of a generally favorable response are usually advantageous. After all, nobody is perfect. If the prospective employers receive only very glowing reports, they are bound to think there is a credibility gap somewhere.

A few times a client has been unhappily surprised with several bad references. These people were dropped from the list of approved references, and we were able to get enough other good replies for our client's use. Persons who do not reply to a reference request will be dropped unless our client knows a plausible reason why we did not hear from them. For example, they are away on a vacation or business trip. We know that some people don't reply because they don't have good things to say!

Note our letter did not ask them to write or to phone. About 20 percent of the replies come by phone. When the references phone us, they have had time to think and will tell us more than they would if we had phoned them at a time convenient for us but not necessarily convenient for them. Over the phone we look for both positives and negatives, knowing that some negatives add credence, and, as a result, they will make better references, as they now have had practice in talking about our client.

Your Approved (Proved) Reference List

Once you have six or more usable references, you should prepare a reference list. This includes the name, title, company, address, and phone number of each person. Company addresses and phones are best, as this is a business matter to be handled during the business day of any prospective employer who actually checks your references. Take this list to each interview. Unless your future boss knows of one or more of your references, you are usually better off not bringing up the matter of references. If you are asked for references, do not give up the list. Instead, ask how your references will be contacted—by letter or by phone. Then dictate or record the names, titles, companies, addresses, *or* phone numbers of the three you would prefer to be checked. Put a mark after each name every time you use it this way. Despite the fact that many requested references may not be checked, it is advisable to spread out the load. The marks will tell you whom you have used the least.

Handling Reference Requests on Applications

Some employment applications ask for references. As stated in the chapter on applications, provide some but request that reference checks be deferred until after an interview develops mutual interest. Put a mark after their name. Again, you are trying to prevent reference requests from becoming a burden on those people who are trying to help you. You want them to continue to sell for you with enthusiasm.

It is for this same reason that you should not list your references on your resume or use the statement "References available on request."

Keep in Touch with Your References

While it is best not to contact references until after you have made the initial check, it is vital to keep in touch with them once they have made your approved list. If asked what happened regarding the "job" that brought on the original request, tell them your investigation of the company raised some questions and you regretfully turned down the offer. Thank them for their help and request permission to use their name again. You will get that permission. Provide them with your resume to help them in handling future inquiries. By all means ask them for introductions, or at least referrals, to companies that might be able to use your services.

Thank References for Your New Job

Finally, after you are in your new job, thank everyone on the list in person or by phone for helping you get the new position. Even if references were never checked by your new affiliation, act as if they were and say you believe their statements about you were a vital factor in your getting the nod. If you ever need them again as references, this will assure you they'll be on your team.

13

Cold Calls
Can Heat Up
Your Future

Just as good salespersons boost their volume by making cold calls on prospects, a smart job hunter will make cold calls on prospective employers. Do not be concerned that a few of them might look down on you for adopting this strategy. Actually, you make them feel important and bolster their egos when you seek their advice.

In fact, many professionals stress this as one of the most important job-search techniques. Some call it advice calls or interviews for information. These names are well chosen, as you will be making cold calls on the pretense of looking for advice or information.

How to Get in the Door

As time permits, you should call on top-level executives at any companies that really interest you as possible employers. First, do the research on each company as described in the chapter on interviewing. Without calling first, walk in and tell the receptionist you would like a few minutes with Mr. Boss to get some advice on that particular industry. If you are not in your hometown, tell where you are from and say you are looking for advice regarding the region. In either case, tell the receptionist you are seeking advice on the industry or the locale from a successful businessman, such as Mr. Boss. You will, of course, know his name as a result of your advance research on the company.

Mr. Boss or his secretary may give some static. If so, ask the receptionist to assure Mr. Boss you are not there to sell him anything, collect for a charity, or apply for a job. You only want a few minutes of advice from a successful businessman. Feed his ego!

What to Tell—What to Ask—What Not to Ask

The odds favor your being given a few minutes. He likes your description of him as a leader in the industry or the area. As soon as you get inside his office, thank him for seeing you. Tell him you are looking for advice on how to obtain a certain position in the area or industry. Say that you are completely inexperienced in job hunting because you have practically been drafted into every job you have had. In three or four sentences tell him about your business background. Then ask him what you should be doing to find the situation you want. He will give you some advice. Some of it may be good and some bad. Of course, you really want him to consider hiring you. If he does not seem to be thinking that way, nudge him a bit by first thanking him for such useful advice and then asking him what companies you should contact for a job. Be sure *not* to ask him for other people to see for advice. That would be an insult, since his advice is *all* you need.

Thank him for each company he tells you to call on. Ask him whom you should see at each one. Would it be permissible for you to use his name as the basis of contact? If he is truly on your side, ask him to introduce you over the phone. You must stress that you will handle the matter from that point on. Later, be sure to write a thank-you letter reporting what happened and asking him to keep you in mind if he hears of something.

Cold Calls Are Worth the Effort—Here's Proof

Cold calls do work. Most clients just don't like the idea. A few absolutely refuse to make them, saying either they are demeaning or they just don't have time for them. I show these clients that they do work and that they work best out of town. Out of town is best because it is easier to get in if you have traveled some distance.

As proof they work, I'll tell you about three different clients who got where they want to be through the judicious use of cold calls. The first, Brad A., loved the small two-city region in which he lived. He had personally built his home and would not consider moving from it. Since the number of companies in the geographical area was small, I decided that the major approach to his market should be cold calls. On his third call he was referred to a fourth company that it was felt could possibly use him. He got the position and the salary he wanted, and he goes home for lunch every day.

Our second example, Carl C., lived in northern Illinois. Unlike Brad A., he *did* want to move. Carl wanted to live in Chicago or one of its suburbs. Obviously, there are plenty of companies in the Chicago area, and the sales-letter technique was picked as the main, though not the only, part of his campaign. His sales letter did produce interviews but none from the better companies in the suburban area he preferred. The company he was most interested in sent him a negative reply. Since it was obviously a form letter from a clerk in the personnel department, a reply by letter or a call on the writer of the negative would have been a waste of time.

Instead, I suggested Carl make a cold call on the president. Although Carl's sales letter had been addressed to the president, we were confident he had never seen it. Carl got to the president by playing up the fact he was from out of town and was an engineering manager for a large corporation the president knew. After a few interviews the president hired Carl as a vice-president in charge of new-product engineering, at a very nice increase in both salary and benefits. This happened more than five years ago. Nobody at the company knows that Carl wrote to it first and was turned down. His letter was thrown away at the time he was rejected.

Finally, you should learn from Phil C.'s experience. Phil was a young Duluth policeman with a brand-new master's degree in public administration and a desire to move to Dallas or Houston. When I learned of this one day before he was to leave for a vacation in those two cities, I suggested he turn his vacation into a job search by making at least two cold calls each day. I told him to take his Duluth police badge with him and show it to each receptionist as a means of introducing himself. He was to explain he was not on Duluth police business but only looking for advice regarding the local area.

Phil not only saw everybody he called on but also got three job offers and several referrals. The best offer was from a distribution center being opened in Houston by a Milwaukee brewer. When Phil told me about it, I created a new gimmick for him. I suggested he phone the man who was to be his new boss with the suggestion that he, Phil, would take a day off from his police job and go to Milwaukee to meet the people at headquarters with whom he would have to write or talk when he was on the new job. Phil was instructed to tell the new boss that meeting those people and seeing how they operated would make him more valuable to the new boss, the company, and himself. The boss was delighted with the thought and gave Phil a $3,000 raise before he actually started in Houston!

Phil's story should prove not only that cold calls find jobs but also that they and all job-search activities will work even better if you can come up with novel ideas on how to get your foot in the door and show you are an innovative or creative self-starter. As you study a company prior to a cold call, consider what the best approach would be and what you should say about yourself in those important three or four sentences describing yourself to Mr. Boss.

It's Easy to Start with a Banker

Do you have cold feet about the prospect of cold calls? Many do. Break the ice by making your first one or two cold calls on bank officers. They see people off the street all the time. They will want to help you in the belief you either are a bank customer or may someday become an important account for them. Also, they do have contacts and knowledge that can be of great help to you.

Cold calls are calls on people you don't know. Another job-finding technique is calling on people you do know or should know, such as your friends and relatives, your business acquaintances, and trade-association managers. Chapter 14 tells you how to travel that route.

14

Using Contacts
for Additional Help

Personal contacts, trade associations, professional organizations, and your college or university are usually good sources of leads to a better job. Because they are involved in the business world or called upon by industry to find capable people, they can greatly enlarge the scope of your search.

Your personal contacts and business people you know— even your relatives—should be utilized to help open doors for you. Start out by making a list of such people. Your Christmas-card list might be a good place to begin. In addition to their names, put their titles, companies, addresses, and phone numbers on paper. Do not leave any persons off the list on the basis they probably have no contacts that could be useful to you. If they are in the business world, they do have contacts. By omitting names, you are only shortchanging yourself. Your next step is to get in touch with them. Do this in person whenever possible. Invite them (one at a time) to lunch. If you are unemployed, the odds are they will pick up the tab!

Take your resume with you. Tell them the type of position you fit and give them more background than appears on the resume. Say that they must know of companies that could possibly use you and *ask for their help.*

Feed Egos—It Pays Off

Do not let pride stand in your way. So many people are afraid to ask for help. When you ask friends or acquaintances for help, you make them feel good by feeding both their egos and service needs. In fact, you can make acquaintances into friends just by asking them to do some favor for you. Even if they can't help, they feel closer to you because you felt you could call on them.

Leave your resume with them as a reminder of your search. Perhaps they'll want more resumes to send to executives they know. Be sure to write them thank-you letters and to follow up with reports on the meetings they arrange for you.

Sample Letter to Personal Contacts

Because of time or geography, you will probably write to more of your personal contacts than you will meet with at their office or over the luncheon table. The letter should enclose a resume and definitely ask for help. It need not go into any details as to why you want to change jobs or why you are unemployed. Instead, the letter seeks their almost immediate help regarding your future. It should be short (more readable), to the point, and personalized. For example:

Jack B. Herald, Vice-President
Acme Manufacturing Corp.
1212 Third Street
San Francisco, CA 94100

Dear Jack:

I'm writing for your help. Per the enclosed resume, I am looking for a new position in sales management. As I have done in the past, I'm the man who can set new sales records in the future. This could be for a company you know. Your help in providing leads to organizations I might fit will be greatly appreciated. I will phone you in a few days.

Thank you,

Joseph P. Weir

P.S. My best to Martha and the kids.

This letter should personally be signed "Joe" rather than "Joseph P. Weir." You should phone him on Tuesday, Wednesday, or Thursday of the week after he receives the letter.

Contact Associations and Professional Organizations

Trade associations, groups of companies within an industry, can be very helpful. They can give you data on their field, and many will provide a listing of their members. Try to talk with their chief paid officers, who can give you some insights into the membership. They should want to serve their members well by telling them of a good person who is available.

The membership of professional organizations is made up of individuals rather than companies. If there is such a group in your field, you should have become a member before you began looking for a job. Your company would probably have paid your dues. If you are unemployed, you might still be able to join but at your own expense. Talk to their chief paid officers and other members to see what they can do to further your job search. They often know of openings in their field and sometimes are called on to help fill them.

How to Approach Your University

Your college or university should be contacted when you get your resumes from the printer. Certainly you should write to the placement office. Include a resume, but in your letter give your degree and year. Occasionally there are calls for older graduates. This is especially true of the better-known business and technical schools. Ask what can be done to help you find a better job.

It is wise to write to the dean of your school and to any favorite professors, as well as to the placement office.

When looking to improve your job situation, you should not overlook any approach that could possibly result in that better job. Never be afraid to ask questions or to ask for help.

15

Selling Yourself
in the Interview

That's what it is all about—selling yourself. Everybody is an individual with a unique personality. Therefore, each person should interview a bit differently from everybody else. In fact, each interview you have should and will be different because the interviewers also have different personalities and needs.

Get Practice Interviews

Obviously, you should try to get as many interviews as possible. Do not turn down an interview because you think the job, the company, the people, or the salary is not right for you. Perhaps you are wrong, and it can be a good match. If the interview does turn out to be a no-go situation, you are still ahead because you will have had the practice of a nonthreatening interview that should improve your personal interviewing skills. In fact, it is advisable at first to interview for jobs that you do not want or that are really not available. Thus, at the start of your job-search campaign, accept what you anticipate to be courtesy interviews from friends or friends of friends. Practice, it is said, makes perfect.

Since your aim in the interview is to sell yourself, you should know what you have to sell. Why will *you* be hired? There are three main reasons why you or anybody else will be hired. Don't ever forget them.

Why You *Will* Be Hired—Your Top Three Selling Points

First, you are qualified to fill the specific needs of the company. Later in this chapter we'll discuss learning what those needs are. We'll also go into more detail on how to sell your ability to fill them.

Second, you are likable. If persons within the company feel they do not like you as a person, you will not be hired. They must agree it will be a pleasure to have you aboard. In fact, if they really like you, they will convince themselves that you are the applicant with the best qualifications. The reverse side of the coin also exists. The most qualified candidates will be turned down as not able to do the job if they are not liked. After all, even interviewers are human beings subject to human frailties and whims.

Your third selling point is your potential. This is a book for executives where potential counts, not order fillers or clerks who will always be order fillers or clerks. When I was merchandising things rather than people, I did not concern myself with the potentialities of the warehouse workers; but no middle- or upper-level manager was hired who did not have both the desire and the probable ability to grow. In fact, we tried to hire as salespeople those we felt could possibly rise through the next four steps to sales vice-president.

A thinking executive will want to hire people who can grow in stature and ability as the company grows, as well as to higher positions within the company, and still not pose any threat to the executive's own future.

Impressions You Should Create

You must create several impressions in the interviewer's mind to sell yourself as qualifying on all three points. I am going to elaborate on them one by one. It is important that you do not assign any rank to these impressions. They are *all* vital. The impressions you should make on each interviewer's mind are the following:

- You are a good manager
- You have true potential
- You are an able negotiator
- You are something of an entrepreneur
- You are qualified to fill the company's needs
- You are a nice person

Good Manager

Many books have been written, and many courses taught, on what a manager is and what a manager does. For the purpose of an interview, you must convince your prospective employer that you are *accustomed* to seeing to it that jobs (notice the plural) are done efficiently. This means you accept responsibility for your actions and for those on your team. You also assume or expect authority to go with responsibility.

As a good manager, you properly motivate people to get into the act. This means your superiors as well as your subordinates become involved if high-level participation is required. Of course, you are able to delegate work to others. However, you are the type of executive who gets in there and pitches to further the action whenever advisable. A good manager is a doer as well as a leader. Represent yourself as a person who joins committees and ends up as the major worker if not the chairperson.

Good managers inspire respect and confidence in others. People come to them with questions or problems. They are known as willing listeners and good advisers. It is more or less understood they can be consulted on matters outside their own sphere of responsibilities in the company. Let the interviewer know that you are such a person.

All too often when I ask clients why a company will hire them, I get the standard answer: "Because I will be a component of profit."

Fine, but how? As a manager, you help produce profits for the company by specific actions on your part. It is up to you to convince the company that you have the ability to help it earn more profits because of what you can do within your own realm or specialty.

True managers or executives will not only help determine a company's operating policies and objectives but will also help guide and control operations to achieve those objectives. They coordinate both people and functions. They can and do make decisions—preferably after analyzing the facts. They consider the development of subordinates to be important to both their future and the company's. At the same time they strive to improve their own capabilities. They are constantly exercising and bettering their own business judgment as overall corporate executives and as specialists within their own field. They can properly represent the company to the outside world, including the general public, competitors, government regulatory agencies, and, of course, customers.

Perhaps, most of all, good managers possess a positive mental attitude. You should radiate a "can do" feeling to the interviewer. Sell yourself to yourself first, then the company. You will be very pleasantly surprised at how much you really *can* do.

It is imperative to think, act, and talk like a manager during the interview. Answering ads and going on practice interviews for jobs you don't want or expect to get will add polish to your presentation when the chips are really down. Be relaxed but alert, friendly and positive, objective rather than subjective, and always enthusiastic.

True Potential

One of the main reasons you will be hired is your potential to grow both with the firm as it grows and within the organization to positions of higher responsibility. If the interviewer doesn't seem to be thinking about your potential, be sure to bring it up yourself. Simply ask about plans for future corporate growth so you will be considered in terms of that growth. Say that you expect to *earn* a more important position in the company. Don't appear as a threat to your prospective boss. In fact, if asked where you see yourself in three to five years with the company, you could say that in those years you will be working hard to help push the interviewer up a few notches in the hopes you will be following right behind. In the interview start building up your future as a crucial subordinate. You want the interviewer to become your sponsoring superior. You are to be his or her crucial subordinate.

Able Negotiator

An able negotiator will understand and follow certain fundamentals or rules to be in a good bargaining position during the interviews. Chapter 16 will go over all of them in detail. It will show you how the interviewer will probably look upon you as being more qualified because you seem to be a tough negotiator. Since you should create the impression of being an able negotiator, I'll give you the rules of negotiating here and show their application in the next chapter.

These rules are simple:

- Never bring up the matter of salary. If interested in you, the interviewer will do so.

- Try not to talk salary until you have learned everything possible about the position and the company.

- Don't bring up fringes. The interviewer will do so.

- Do not get involved in any talk regarding fringes until the salary has been discussed.

- Do not accept any offer on the spot. This is your life, your career, and it requires time for adequate reflection.

Entrepreneur

Another impression to create is that of an entrepreneur rather than a job applicant. As an entrepreneur, you are selling your services to prospective buyers. Nobody makes a sale *every time*. Since your world will not come to an end if you don't get a particular job offer, you can be relaxed and friendly. As an entrepreneur, you will hold your head high at all times. Make it clear that you have had other interviews and have still more scheduled. While you will never use an offer from one company as a bargaining lever to increase the offer from another, always let it be known when you get each offer that you do have others and need time to make a true career decision. After all, this is to be your lifetime employer.

To help you think in positives only, I'm going to ask you to read the preceding sentence one more time. Note, I did not say, "After all, this is to be your last job change," which has a negative connotation because it implies that you have made many such changes and can be expected to move again after being hired by this company.

An entrepreneur is always in control of options. If you are employed and looking for a better job, one of your options is, of course, your present position. In addition, you also have all the options of the unemployed job searcher, who has interviews already scheduled, others yet to be arranged, companies who are interested, perhaps some offers, and definitely has qualifications that will land a job.

Qualified to Fill the Company's Needs

Obviously, you must show you are qualified to fill the company's needs. Your business experience, accomplishments, promotions, interview kit, knowledge of the industry and the company, and your ability to speak in the jargon of the industry all help to show you are qualified. By setting realistic career goals for yourself, you know you are qualified.

To come across as qualified to fill the needs, you must do your homework to learn everything possible about the company, the officers, the industry, and the expected requirements for the job. Ask as many questions over the telephone before the interview as you can. Talk to the person who will interview you, or anybody else you can reach. Your only concern is to avoid letting them interview *you* over the phone. Remember, always sound like a nice person—a happy individual.

Nice Person

Last but certainly not least, you must come across as a nice person—somebody that will be liked personally. That should not be difficult for anybody. The best way to come across in an interview as a nice person is to be a happy one. Be sure to smile during every interview. Adopt a relaxed but attentive, friendly, positive, and happy manner.

Try to hold yourself at the interviewer's level. Be respectful but do not feel intimidated. After all, you are an entrepreneur with other possibilities to consider.

The nice person does not knock anything or anybody, talking in positives only. Any negative brought up can be held against you. For the same reason avoid controversial subjects and do not divulge any confidences.

A nice person—the one who will be hired—acts a bit like a guest during an interview. Certainly you will not smoke unless it is obvious there are no objections to your doing so. Joe M. lost an offer because he "stunk up my receptionist's office and then proceeded to stink up mine with his terrible cigars."

Be alert and sincere. All too often the small talk during the first quarter hour of an interview gives the immediate impression on which hiring decisions are made. A straightforward, confident manner will pay off.

Preparation for the Interview—Homework

Before the actual interview, you will have done extensive research on the company at the library and possibly with the company's competitors and customers. Your best source for such information is the latest annual report or the Form 10-K filed with the Securities and Exchange Commission. Perhaps your broker can provide the report. You can write a short letter to the corporate secretary requesting a copy of the annual report. Say you are thinking of investing in the company—you are really thinking of investing your career in them. Libraries in large cities often have annual reports or 10-Ks.

Read every word in either the report or 10-K. You are looking for data that give you background on the company. A financial person should study the balance sheets and operating statements carefully. Develop questions to ask during the interview to show you have done your homework and are thinking about the company's financial situation. Obviously, the person doing the hiring identifies with the company and will favor the candidate who shows knowledge and interest in the company.

If you are not a financial person, you should still look at the figures to get a feeling of the size and strengths or weaknesses of the organization. Know the trend of both sales and profits, and memorize last year's.

Officers and Directors

Find out something about the officers and directors. You should know at least the age, education, and business background of the officers who could be your boss or your boss's boss. The research librarian can help you with this, but first try Dun & Bradstreet's *Reference Book of Corporate Managements* or some of the *Who's Who* books. If possible, learn the hobbies of those who may be important to your future with the company. You may have common interests that can help sell you and make them like you.

Company Products and Services

Learn as much as you can about the company's products or services. If you don't know what the company does for a living, don't go to the interview! Learn about its marketplace and how it sells to that market. By marketplace I am referring to the general type of clientele, such as consumers, manufacturers, or department stores—not the names of customers, such as General Motors or A&P. Learn everything you can about the whole industry, with emphasis on the company's competitors.

Make Up Questions to Ask

As you study the company and the people, prepare a list of intelligent questions to ask during the interview. Make sure the person on the other side of the desk knows that you have done your homework and have made up the questions in advance. The questions can be on one or more three-by-five-inch cards or in a pocket-size notebook. When the discussion covers one of your questions, pull out the list and check off the question you no longer need to ask. This shows that you have done your homework. When you ask one of your prepared questions, finger the written word or point to it with your pen in preparation for checking it off.

Your questions should be written in an outline form, using only one or two words per question. That way you won't be reading questions instead of looking the interviewer in the eye as you ask for the information. These queries should do more than just show that you have studied the company. They should enable you to bring out some of your qualifications that specifically fit the company.

Preselect Data on Yourself for Each Interview

While studying the company, you will of course be thinking of what you can offer it. I am going to be arbitrary now and insist that you be prepared for each interview with three things in your background to weave into the conversation. These three qualities or experiences should match the company's needs or activities.

Your Interview Kit

If possible, bring your interview kit (see chapter 11) or portfolio to the interviews to help prove your background. It should be changed from interview to interview to elaborate on the three qualities mentioned above.

You can make or break yourself depending on how you use an interview kit. Bear in mind that it has one purpose only: to close the credibility gap arising in all too many interviews of late. The head of one of the largest (franchise) employment-agency operations in the United States got national publicity with his statement that lies are necessary in interviews because the interviewers these days expect everybody to lie at least a little. Later a professor at Harvard Business School was written up in newspapers and magazines for teaching his M.B.A. candidates to lie under certain circumstances. All the more reason for an interview kit! But, reread chapter 11 before using it the first time.

Have Answers Ready for Expected Questions

Another way to prove you are qualified for the particular job is to be prepared to answer questions that you expect to be asked. Think up such questions as you study the company. Know the answers you should give. Also be prepared for a host of questions that are generally asked in interviews. Some are asked to create stress in your mind. They are used as a means of finding out how the candidate will react when under stress on the job. Figure 27 is a list of questions that have been asked again and again. Practice on them, developing answers that show a positive mental attitude coupled with an open, honest person. Many of these questions do not have a single right answer. The answers you give should, in most instances, be tailored to the particular opening under discussion, the interviewer, and/or the company. Some of the questions listed may not fit your circumstances or the job and therefore won't be asked of you.

As an example of tailoring an answer, there is nothing wrong with answering the question on short-range objectives by saying, "To get this job with the Smith Company."

Your biggest weaknesses should be those the interviewer could consider as strengths, such as impatience at times to get the job done, perfectionism, or being overly results-oriented. Try to turn all negatives into positives.

Some questions require negative replies, and you should give them. It is permissible to describe the least competent boss you ever had, but it would be wrong to divulge the name. If asked to do so, reply that you would rather not, since you are being critical. When did you last break the law? Probably the last time you drove a car.

A true answer to the question about your health could be "I don't remember the last day I took off because of sickness."

In a practice interview I was once asked my net worth. Since I feel no interviewer is entitled to such information, I said, "Why do you ask? Is there a chance for me to buy an equity position here?" At first he almost stammered. Then he did start trying to sell me an interest. I then learned there was enough wrong with the company that I wouldn't have accepted a position, much less bought in. Perhaps a better answer would be evasive but truthful, such as "Not enough to gloat over, but enough so as not to lose sleep." You do not have to strip yourself naked by answering all questions to get a job. A firm that insists on knowing too much is probably not the one you should join.

The best question you can be asked is: What can you do for us? Your answer will be keyed to showing how you can fill the company's needs, how your qualifications agree with the corporate activities.

If you have any doubts about the right answer to some of these questions, ask a friend who is active in the business world for guidance. Hopefully, your friend will be experienced in interviewing and will have asked the same or similar questions of applicants.

Warnings Regarding Interviews

No Time-Outs or Recesses

There are certain warnings to keep in mind concerning behavior at interviews. To begin with, you should realize there is no time-out during an interview. As long as you are with any employee of the company, you are, in effect, being interviewed. The receptionist mentioned earlier complained to the boss before Joe M. got into the boss's office. It is possible this made the boss more aware of Joe's cigar than would otherwise have been the case. A secretary or receptionist cannot assure your being hired but can very possibly turn the cards against you.

How to Dress Properly

One would think it would be wasting your time (and mine) to warn you to dress properly for an interview. I have learned it is wrong to assume that people of otherwise good sense can be depended upon to always use their common sense in this regard. Even in today's somewhat liberal times, a man with a beard and moustache should appear clean shaven for interviews. All that facial adornment may well serve to kill his chances with a majority of the companies. All too often we've been told by clients that the company had better take them as they are, or they don't want to join it. If you want to cut your chances for getting the right job by more than 50 percent, there is nothing I can do about it. At the very least, I suggest you tell each interviewer that you would be willing to remove the excess hair if it would help get you the offer. Tom C. had what I can only describe as a beard shaped by his religion. It was very much out of the ordinary. After a few interviews in which he scored very poorly, he did shave it off. In very little time he received three or four offers and accepted one in a city where he wanted to live. When he came back to see me for a review a year later, he was wearing a modern beard.

Fig. 27

What are your long-range objectives?

Your short-range objectives?

How do you rate your abilities?

Describe your present (or last) boss.

What are your major strengths?

Your biggest weaknesses?

How come you've been unemployed so long?

What did (or do) you like best about your job?

What did (or do) you dislike about your job?

Define the background of success.

How have you made more dollars for a company?

Why do you want to work for us?

Tell me all about yourself.

What did you do at your last job? What were your responsibilities?

Why did you leave your last job?

If you could have made one suggestion to management, what would it
    have been?

What have you done that you're proud of?

Describe the best boss you ever had.

Describe the least competent boss you ever had.

Tell me about the status of your health in recent years.

What kinds of things bother you the most?

What else should I know about your qualifications?

What else would you like to know about this job?

Have you ever stolen anything?

Do you ever lie?

When did you last break the law?

Favorite alcoholic beverage?

How much do you drink?

Have you ever received counseling or psychotherapy?

What do you like to do in your spare time?

Why were you passed over for promotion?

What is your net worth?

Why never married?

Why did your business fail?

Why did you lose your job?

What can you do for us?

Give me three or four words your spouse would use to describe you.

Is there anything else you want to tell me about yourself?

Your clothes should be modern but not mod. Of course, I don't need to tell you they should be clean and well pressed and your shoes shined! Always wear a business suit unless you have been lucky enough to determine in advance how the people in the company dress. If so, dress for the interview like they dress on the job. Bill J. was a very good salesman, but he couldn't sell himself, since he interviewed in flashy clothes. "This is me," he said when I admonished him. I told him he could be himself after he had a job and could afford to do so. Both have happened.

Women should wear a dress or a suit for their interviews. Please, no slacks. We are not trying to make sex objects out of our female clients when we tell them not to wear a scarf or a dress buttoned to the neck, but some interviewers will think they are trying to hide unsightly features or are too prim and prudish to function well with others in the company. On the other hand, a woman should not show up dressed for a party or in stiletto-style high heels or boots.

Perhaps this story will help you understand the importance of dressing right for your interviews. Some time ago when engineers of all types were in big demand, Edward B. came to us for help. He was a graduate chemical engineer and had been seeking a job for more than four months on his own. It wasn't long before we had him going on several interviews, but he never received so much as a nibble of an offer. We went over interviewing techniques with him again and again. We spent hours in role playing. While he was far from being a master interviewer, he certainly was not so bad that he should be unable to get a position in his field under the market conditions then existing. One day, after he had just left my office, the receptionist phoned and asked whether I had ever seen Ed with his hat and coat on. I thanked her for the tip and arranged to walk out to the reception area with Ed at the conclusion of our next meeting. I watched Ed put on his overcoat. It was the maxicoat to beat all maxicoats. It almost reached down to the top of his shoes. Then he put on his hat. It was held up by his ears, since they turned outward under the weight of the hat. Evidently, his attire was called to the attention of prospective employers by their receptionists. After a visit to a clothing store, Ed accepted an offer developing and testing new food products.

A Drink at an Interview Meal?

If the interviewer takes you to lunch or dinner, it is not a recess or time-out. Your social graces, conversational abilities, *and* technical qualifications will be studied. Remember to be friendly, happy, alert, sincere, and not a big drinker. This does not mean you should refuse a drink if offered. Such a refusal can stamp you as unfriendly. Accept a drink offer by saying "I'll be happy to join you." Order a mixed drink, such as vodka and tonic, scotch and soda, etc. Then nurse that drink through the whole meal. If a second drink is suggested, say you are happily working on the one you have. Warning: Don't order a small and powerful drink, such as a martini. Instead, order a drink you do not like so that it will be easier to stretch it out.

Don't Give the Store Away

Avoid becoming a free consultant. It is possible to tell an interviewer so much about how a particular job should be done or how a problem can be solved that it is no longer necessary to hire you or anybody else for the position.

Don't Be Critical

You can also talk yourself out of an offer by criticizing something that is being done. I have found that my engineering clients are the most likely to offer free consulting services in the form of constructive criticism. Jack K. is one mechanical engineer who received an offer by not talking himself out of it. The president of a printing company took Jack into the plant to show off his operation. Stopping by a massive piece of printing machinery, he asked Jack's opinion of it. Jack told me—not the president—it was an old clunker whose output could be increased by making many changes. Although Jack felt the company would be far better off replacing it with modern equipment, he told the president it was a very interesting machine and that he would like a chance to really study it. Just then the president was paged for a phone call. Before leaving for his office, he asked the plant manager to show Jack the rest of the shop. The plant manager had seen Jack and the president looking at the machine and asked Jack what he had said to the president about it. When Jack told him, the manager laughed, put his arm around Jack's shoulder and said, "You're going to get the job! That darn machine is the boss's pride and joy. He refuses to hear anything bad about it."

Therefore, if you are shown a machine, a business form, or anything else the firm does or uses, and asked, "Can you improve on this?" your answer should intimate that it does look interesting and that you can, if given time to really study it and how it fits in with other activities of the company, come up with some interesting modifications. That way you do not insult anybody by knocking something that person may be proud of. Also, you are not hurting feelings by solving in a few seconds a problem that they could not handle after trying for weeks, months, or even years.

How to Control the Interview

You should be able to *control* your interviews. Control does not mean you will be the one to decide what will be discussed. The interviewer will exercise that prerogative. Control means you won't say too much. You control your end of the interview by telling only what you want known. Before you answer any question, think for a moment. After you do answer the question, do not blurt out additional information because the interviewer is sitting there waiting for you to say more. Ask a question about the position, the people, or the company to fill the void of silence.

Don't be intimidated. If questions are fired at you fast and furiously, answer each one properly before going on to the next. You certainly can ask to have a question repeated. This is especially true if it was asked while you were answering a previous one. The rush may be part of a stress interview.

It is possible you will be interviewed by more than one person at a time. Field each question separately. Do not allow yourself to become disconcerted if A asks you a question while you're answering B's query. If you do hear A's question and it does relate to what you are discussing, include an answer to A in your reply, now addressed to both persons. If the question opens a new field, or if you really did not hear it, do not lose your stride in replying as you planned. Just nod to A and continue satisfying B. Then you can return to A and either repeat the question or request to have it repeated. Explain that you did not hear it, since you were talking to B when it was asked.

To repeat: Control the interview by telling only what you want known. There is an old saying that many sales are killed by the jawbone of an ass. You are selling yourself in an interview and certainly don't want to kill your sale that way. Actually, most people would be better off if they spent more time listening than talking in interview situations. Talk little, listen long.

You should realize that you and the interviewers have similar yet conflicting aims. Theirs is to learn as much as possible about you but to tell you only enough about the job and the company to draw you out and still sell you on the position in case they decide you are the person they want. You, on the other hand, want to learn everything possible about the job and the company but to say only what you want known for them to make you an offer.

When you are asked to "tell me all about yourself," don't waste the interviewer's time or yours—don't kill your chances—by saying too much. Don't talk about your place of birth, parents, early schooling, spouse, children, style of living, etc., etc. Instead, talk about your qualifications for the job.

If you feel you need more information about the specific requirements of the job, start out by saying, "Of course, I want to tell you about myself. But if you will tell me something about this job, I can save you time by showing how I fit." Most interviewers can see the wisdom of this reply and will begin telling you what points you want to sell. A few may react differently and hold their cards close to their chest. If so, you can say, "If you will tell me what you are looking for, I will do something I'm sure nobody else has ever done. I will tell you the parts I fit and confess to the parts I do not fit." Hopefully, you can shrug off the latter by stating your ability to pick them up and handle them after only a few days or weeks: "After all, with my background I'll soon be handling them as if I had been doing them all my life."

Ending the Interview

Your obvious aim in an interview is to get an offer. At the executive level, offers are rarely given in the first interview. Therefore, you want to end the interview on a positive note with a definite understanding of what is to happen next and when. Interviews usually come to an end when the interviewers rather than the candidates call them to a halt. They will probably verify your interest in the position and then come up with the expected statement that you will hear from them in a few weeks. That is the time for you to really prove you are not only a good manager but also an entrepreneur. Pull out a pocket-size notebook with a calendar and say something like "Two weeks from now is Tuesday, February twentieth. I'd like to call you on that day if I have not yet heard from you." Their reply will probably be "Don't call us, we'll call you." You should then say you have other interviews scheduled in various cities and will be hard to reach in the next few weeks. If employed, you can add that you will also be doing some traveling for your company during that time and therefore would like to call back at or around February 20. Ask them to suggest another date if they seem reluctant.

Knowing that other companies are interviewing you makes you more valuable in the minds of interviewers. It is another one of your selling points.

Make it a practice to phone all interviews on the agreed dates. The fact that you have set a definite date enables you to handle your other interviews with a free mind. If you left it up to the interviewers to contact you at any time within a few weeks, you would begin wondering why they had not called after a very few days. By the second week your wonder would turn to worry. I have no statistics on this, but I know for a fact that most interviewers do not call or write within two weeks. All too often it takes them three or four weeks. Arranging to call them will relieve your mind and impress them.

Almost immediately after each interview, fill out the Interview Report form shown in figure 28. It is important, as it summarizes the interview for you, making follow-ups and second or third interviews much easier. It will cement in your mind what did occur. Equally important, it will help you in future contacts with the company, including the thank-you/sales letter.

Always Follow Up with a Thank-You/Sales Letter

As soon as possible after every interview, send the interviewer a combination thank-you/sales letter. *This is very important.* The aim

Fig. 28

INTERVIEW REPORT FORM

Date of Interview _____ 19 ____ Interview Source _____

Company _____

Address _____ City & State _____

Individual _____ Title _____

Other Persons Seen _____

Position Discussed _____

Duties of Position _____

Products/Services of Company _____

How Sold _____ $ Sales of Company _____

Conversation Summary (continue on back of page, if necessary): _____

_____

_____

_____

_____

_____

_____

_____

_____

Did you volunteer too much? _____

_____

Result of Interview _____

_____

Planned Follow-up Action _____

Attach Copy of Your Sales/Thank-you Letter to This Report.

of this book is to give you an edge over competition looking for the same job. This letter really puts you above the others who do not bother to write after interviews. When I teach this to clients, almost all tell me they have never received such a letter after interviewing applicants or received only a few. One client, who had lost his position as president of a medium-sized truck line, volunteered that he had received only one such letter in several hundred interviews. "I'll bet you hired him," I said. "That's the man who got my job!"

Your thank-you/sales letters should go to the persons in charge of your interviews, with carbons or a separate letter to everybody else who met with you. Start out by thanking them for seeing you. Do not thank them for taking time out of their "busy schedules" to interview you. Such meetings are part of their jobs. In addition, this statement demeans you and the value of your time. Next, your letter should say something good about the company and/or its people. Now you can repeat your great interest in both the position and the organization. State that you can do the job. Go on to prove you are the person for the position by using any or all of what follows. To begin with, you can remind them of facts in your business experience and training that closely fit their requirements. In effect, you are now recalling to them the information you used to sell yourself during the interview. Be sure to remind them of facts about you that seemed of particular interest. Perhaps you have had some new thoughts since then. Here is your chance to say what you forgot to bring out in person. Finally, you might *very carefully* rebut any arguments they may have against you. Unless you have a good rebuttal, you are better off not reminding them of any doubts. However, a rebuttal with logic can turn their thinking around to your benefit.

The following is only one of several instances of a rebuttal in a thank-you/sales letter actually securing offers. An old friend of mine phoned several years ago asking for help in finding a salesman to later become a sales manager. At that time I had two clients who I felt could fill the bill based on personality match, sales ability, sales-management potentiality, and a familiarity with his types of customers. I arranged for them to phone for interviews. Bill J., the flashy dresser mentioned earlier in this chapter, had the first interview. My friend was not too impressed. I had told Bill to wear a suit. He did not. Then John C. had his interview. John came to my office directly from the meeting. He wanted that job very much but felt my friend would turn him down because he was only twenty-three years old. So I helped John write a thank-you/sales letter with particular emphasis on the advantages of hiring a young man who had already been proved as a salesman and could easily be taught how the *company* wanted its sales manager to function. The next day my friend phoned to tell me he had been unhappy with John's youth until he had received the letter. He insisted on reading me the paragraph in the letter about the advantages of youth! He hired John, and to this day my friend keeps telling me how well John is doing. John is now national sales manager.

Your thank-you/sales letter should close on a positive note. For example, "I look forward to phoning you February 20 with my calendar in hand so we can arrange our next meeting."

As explained in the chapter on handling positive replies, you should be paid expenses for your out-of-town interviews. Many companies will pay this by cash or check while you are there. Others will ask you to bill them. Do not make that billing a part of your thank-you/sales letter. This is a selling letter that should remain on their desk to remind them of you. It should not be part and parcel of a request for money. In fact, if you put money matters in the letter, it will have to go to accounts payable. Make the invoice a separate piece of paper. Since the transportation is usually paid in advance or charged directly to the company, it is sometimes better not to invoice the company for small out-of-pocket expenses until after the last meeting. Or, better yet, when you are in your new job with that company.

Use Rejections for Critiques on Your Interviewing Practices

This book has been telling you to go on every interview possible because you need the practice or because the job itself may be traded up or actually be better than you had reason to expect.

Of course, you will not always sell yourself (get the offer) in some of your practice interviews or even in some of the interviews involving a job you really want. You can and should turn some of these rejections to your advantage by getting ideas on how you come across in an interview.

Phone the interviewers who tell you the job went to somebody else. Immediately put them at ease by saying you are not calling about the job you did not get but about advice. Ask them how you come across in an interview. "What do I do right? More important, what do I do wrong?"

Note that you are not asking why you were turned down. You are asking for help, and the odds are very strong you will get helpful advice. The sooner you phone after the interview and the rejection, the better chance you will have of being remembered and getting the information you want.

Get a Referral If You Don't Want the Job

If, during particular interviews, you decide you do not want the job *for reasons other than salary,* you should use the occasion to get a referral to another potential employer. In such instances, call a halt by telling the interviewers you are not the right person for the job. Go on to say that you like them and their company and believe you can be of help. It so happens that you know a person who you believe would fit their needs very well!

"Who is that?" will be their immediate reaction.

"This man is employed, and he probably won't like my giving his name out like this to you or any other company. Let me phone him first. I promise either he or I will get back to you."

Since you are going out of your way for them, the interviewers are under some sort of obligation to you. Now is the time to ask for names of one or more companies that could possibly use your particular talents. After you get the names of the companies, ask which individuals in those companies you should contact. Then ask them if they would be kind enough to introduce you over the phone. Assure them all you want is a short introduction—you will carry the ball from there.

You then owe the interviewers a call regarding the man you are referring to them and the results of your contacting the companies to which they referred you. The latter is easy—just summarize what happened. Regarding the man for their job, tell them a bit about him and that they can expect a phone call (as actually arranged) very soon. If you did not have an actual person in mind, or if your man was not at all interested in the job, say that your man is not interested only because he recently was promoted, started a new job, or moved away, or give any other plausible reason why your efforts did not pan out. Of course, you will keep your eyes and ears open for a person to fill the interviewers' needs, just as you know they'll keep you in mind for a position with their company or with another firm they may learn can use a person with your abilities.

To summarize, go into each interview knowing why you should be hired and what you have to sell. Create all the proper impressions relative to your personality, your qualifications, and your understanding of the company and its needs. It is often said that talk is cheap. Talking too much in interviews is very expensive—it can cost you job offers. Your research before each interview session will enable you to talk correctly.

In advance of each interview, our clients often reread their notes on how to present themselves. Many claim this effort is extremely rewarding. Although this chapter could not be personalized for you, it is suggested you reread it before each of your interviews.

16

How to Negotiate
a Good Salary

You should always hold your head high during interviews and negotiations. As discussed in the chapter on interviewing, as an entrepreneur you are also a tough negotiator. Don't be afraid to be tough. It's your life and your future being determined. If prospective employers obviously think you are too tough a negotiator, say something like: "Mr. Smith, you think I'm a tough negotiator. Good. The person in this position must properly represent the Smith Company all the time. He will never be a good representative for your company if he can't properly represent himself." This will almost always bring them back to your side. In fact, it will make you a better candidate in their eyes.

How to Live Within the Rules of Negotiations

Chapter 15 merely outlines the fundamental rules of negotiating to follow if you are to get the optimum salary. Now we will discuss these in depth. To begin with, and this is easy, you should not be the one to bring up salary in the interview. If interested in you, the interviewer will do so. Second rule, if it is brought up at or near the beginning of the interview, *try* in as nice a way as possible to avoid discussing it. The matter of dollars is brought up early only to see how cheaply you can be got or to find out whether your expectations fit the salary range. A definite figure from you at this stage may eliminate you from consideration, whereas you might have been able to discuss a more important position in the company had you been able to sell your qualifications before getting into the question of salary. Stating a figure early in the interview can also hurt your bargaining power. If you state a low figure, you'll never get up near the top of the range.

How can you avoid answering salary questions if they come up too soon? You should, in a friendly manner, state that you would very much like to talk dollars after learning more about the requirements of the job. Immediately follow up with a question about the work or the company in the hopes of avoiding the salary issue. For example, "Mr. Smith, I believe salary should be based on the requirements of the job—its responsibilities." Before the interviewer has a chance to insist upon talking salary now, ask something specific about the job, perhaps one of the questions you prepared in advance of the interview.

Another courteous "nonreply" to a premature question regarding your salary needs or history could be: "Mr. Smith, I assure you if the two of us decide I'm the person for this job, we can't possibly have a problem over salary"; or, "Mr. Smith, while salary is not unimportant, it is not so vital to me as the prospect of joining a successful, important, growing company like the Smith Company. I know you pay proper salaries, and I'm sure my earnings will increase as I do my part to help your growth."

If an answer to the salary question is still insisted upon, give one rather than lose any chance of being hired. Tell the interviewer your compensation in your last or your present job even if you are asked for your salary requirements rather than your present salary. After all, it will be assumed you are not going to change jobs without increasing your earnings.

Your third rule of negotiating is simple to follow: Never introduce the subject of fringes. This is one matter the interviewer will surely bring up. In fact, fringes may be brought up too early in the interview. This leads to the fourth rule: Do not become involved in a discussion of fringes until after the salary has been set. A few clients have evaded this rule and learned to regret it. The interviewers in each case told my clients about the beautiful fringes awaiting them. I could only tell those few erring clients that it is impossible to eat fringes and the offers they would receive would be too low. Then I'd hear, "But he knows what I'm earning now. He will offer me even more than that." All the clients who violated rule number four did receive offers of less than their present or last earnings. It was very obvious the interviewers were playing up fringes because they could not offer adequate pay.

Rule number five tells you never to accept an offer at the time it is made. You have every right to be given a chance to think it over. Say that you are very interested in the offer, you like the company and the people, but you want time to think it over, especially in light of the other offers you have. You should say this even if you don't have any other offers. Please do not attempt to raise a bid by saying that somebody else has offered more. It will only be resented and you may well lose the offer. Instead, imply that you are going to accept the offer but need time to confirm your own thoughts on it. This is a one-time career decision and thus cannot be made without due consideration. You are asking for one or two weeks to think.

How to Accept the Offer

If you decide to take the offer, don't wait for the one or two weeks to go by before phoning to accept. Instead, phone rather thrilled that you have accepted the offer and let it be known you really cannot wait to start your new career. However, if you are employed, you should have already made it known you need thirty days before you can start because of work you are doing for your present employer. Interviewers like to hear this because it indicates you are both important and conscientious. Chances are you would not leave the new job either without giving adequate notice.

How to Renegotiate an Offer

Perhaps you will want to renegotiate for more money. A few days after an offer is made, phone for another appointment to go over some matters that are bothering you. If the company is out of town, you can do the renegotiating over the telephone. Either way, express your happiness over the fact that the company does want you. However, you believe you will do so well that a salary of $X would, in your opinion, be much more in line. In fact, if you could start at the higher figure, you would be so gung ho that you would be worth much more than $X.

I can positively state that a great majority of my clients whom I told to renegotiate like this did get all or most of the renegotiated figure they asked for. The chapter on answering ads told you how Dave K. renegotiated an $18,500 offer to $27,500. That is our record for increases on a percentage basis. There were bigger ones dollarwise in cases involving much higher original offers. Just two days ago Jim A. phoned to tell me the offer he had expected and wanted most had just come in, but there was one major problem. It was too low! He really had expected at least $3,000 more. He acted as if his whole world had fallen apart. I suggested he phone the company to say he would start at the figure offered but $250 a month more would make him produce as if he were getting double that amount. The company not only agreed to pay the additional $3,000 but also promised to give him a salary review in six months rather than in the customary one year after beginning employment.

Joyce M. talked to my associate regarding an offer she had just received. She wanted the job badly because it fit her career requirements very well and she was anxious to make a change. However, the offer was only $1,000 more than she was earning. The prospective employer knew her income and used it as a base for the offer. Joyce was told to explain that a $1,000 increase wasn't worth the gamble involved in starting new with a company. She asked for $3,000 more than the offer and got it.

We had not found that job for Joyce. She had used her personal contacts. She had asked them to keep their eyes and ears open for a possible position for her. However, we had told her to talk to everybody and anybody who she felt could help her. More important—and the subject of this chapter—we told her how to get more money on an offer she was going to turn down.

You Have Every Right to Negotiate

There must be thousands of offers rejected every day or accepted at a nonnegotiated figure because the job hunters did not think they had the right to negotiate. Nonsense! If a store clerk shortchanged you, you'd call attention to it. Look on a too-low offer as a shortchange and negotiate for yourself as a business person would negotiate a deal for a company.

Some interviewers are too nice. They let the applicants leave thinking they are going to get an offer when, in truth, the interviewers have reservations they are reluctant to express. Some are afraid to say no, but you would be far better off if they did so that you could continue looking rather than spend time (and wishful thinking) waiting for an offer that won't come. Removing the job from your list of possibilities would release your time, energy, and thinking for more productive job-search activities.

Recognize a Buy Signal

Let's assume that instead of asking you questions regarding salary early in the interview—and coming up with a dollar figure—the prospective employer does so at the end of the first interview or in a later interview. This is not to find out whether you are in the company's financial ball park. It is really a buy signal. You should answer in a way that continues to sell yourself.

A Ploy to Bring Out the Interviewer's Doubts

If, and only if, you have real confidence in your ability as a self-salesperson, should you answer a "dollar sign" question by saying, "Then you agree. I am the person for the job." The reply will be "Yes, but . . ." You want to know about any doubts the interviewer might have so you can dispel them and strike out for more than was planned. You might have created a misconception about yourself by a statement you made during the interview.

How and When to Bring Up Dollars

After you have corrected any misconceptions (or in immediate response to a dollar-sign question late in the interview), you are ready to strike out for the maximum pay possible for that position. Since all during the interview you have been thinking about what the job should pay, you can reply to the salary question by saying, "Mr. Smith, I have been making a personal survey of the market for positions like this. My survey has resulted in quite a few interviews and a few job offers. Based on these interviews and offers, it is clear a person in this position should be able to earn somewhere between X dollars and Y dollars."

$X should be a figure that would entice you into accepting the offer. $Y should be anywhere from $4,000 to $10,000 higher. Without giving the interviewer a chance to react verbally to your preceding statement, talk right on and say, "I believe I am worth Y dollars to you because . . ." What follows should be a reminder of those things in your background that seemed the most appealing or to best fit the needs of the company. In other words, now the chips are really down, and you are giving an educated recap of how you are the best person for the job.

If the Offer Is Too Low

Instead of asking your price, some interviewers may come up with their own. It may be less than the $X you have mentally set for the position. First, sit still for a count of ten. Look them in the eye. They'll know you are not happy with the offer, and they may squirm a bit or raise the ante. If they don't say anything, tell them about your personal survey and the results indicating that a person in that position should be able to earn at least $X. You should not talk about $Y, since you will not get that much from these interviewers at the beginning. You can remind them of the facts about you they like.

If Mr. Smith tells you he will not or cannot pay the $X that came up when you told him of your survey, say, "This is what is being paid today for positions of this responsibility. I wouldn't be fair to you, the Smith Company, myself, or my family if I accepted this position for less than X dollars. Surely, you can raise your sights, Mr. Smith." Say that last sentence as if it were a question.

Hopefully, he will come up to your figure. If not, gracefully tell him you would like to keep the door open. You do want to join Mr. Smith and his company. Suggest he contact you if he is unable to find the type of person he wants at his price. "I'll come running back to talk some more."

If the Offer Is Higher Than You're Thinking

Perhaps you come across so well in an interview, so capable, and so desirable that you are offered more than you expected. Don't be afraid to smile. As you smile, look the interviewer in the eye and say, "That's exactly what I thought this position should pay!" You are certainly starting out on the right foot with your new boss—complete agreement.

Fringes

Once you have an offer worth considering, you and the interviewer will naturally get into a discussion of fringes. Our tax laws and changes in the economy have, in my opinion, made what used to be considered fringe benefits or perquisites (perks) an expected part of each person's salary. Would you accept an offer from a company that did not provide hospitalization insurance for you and your dependents? I'm sure you would not. One sickness or accident these days can cost many years of salary.

The point is, some companies offer better coverage for their employees than others. Major medical or catastrophe insurance is no longer a fringe—it is a necessity. At any rate, most companies do offer some benefits. Perhaps the company itself pays some of these directly to you rather than buy insurance protection. Either way, you can show yourself to be something of a manager if you ask the interviewer to give you brochures or manuals on the coverage. Say you'll study them and come back with any questions you have.

You can do the same regarding profit sharing, pension plans, and stock options. These have been written up for the IRS as well as for the employees. Say that you can save the interviewer's time by reading, rather than by being told, about the plans. Actually, you will learn the facts better, since the interviewer might have some misconceptions about the various company plans.

Handling Moving Expenses

Definitely not a fringe, but of great importance to you, is the cost of moving if a move is necessary. The company should pay for it. If the interviewer has not brought the matter up, you should—but only after the salary has been agreed upon. Do not ask *whether* the company will pay for moving your furniture, your car, yourself, and your family. Instead, make it known you expect those expenses to be covered. This could be done by saying, "Do you want me to get bids on moving, or do you have a mover the company prefers to use?" The interviewer will get the message, and the proper arrangements can then be made.

If you decide to accept a new position with a company that will not pay toward your move, the IRS will help you. Such expenses, within certain limitations, are tax deductible. You should obtain complete information from the IRS before you start your move. Write for its publication 521.

Family Visits—House-Hunting Trips

Many companies will allow you to visit your family (usually every other weekend) if you can't move it until a few months after you start your new job. They will pay your transportation costs and sometimes allow you a special long weekend. Perhaps they will bring your spouse to your new city to help hunt for a new home or apartment for the family. They will put you in touch with a reliable realtor and advise you regarding neighborhoods, transportation, and special living conditions in the area. This trip will usually be in lieu of one of your weekend trips back home.

Financing Your New Home

As the price of real estate has gone up, the number of companies agreeing to help new employees with the purchase of their homes seems to have gone down. However, your new employer may well help you with your new home by introducing you to a bank or savings and loan association to get financing. Your company may also give you a short-term loan to help swing a house purchase. Remember to keep it short term. It is not advisable to take a mortgage from your employer.

Interim Living Expenses

Most companies will pay room and board for their new executive-level employees for 90 to 120 days if, for good reason, these new executives must delay their move. It does take time to sell a home. Perhaps the children have a few months left of their school semester.

So the company arranges for the use of a motel room on a monthly basis. A few of our clients have been placed in corporation-owned apartments. Since these contained cooking facilities, they received free rent but nothing toward meals.

The president and, as usual, the IRS have been trying to cut down on the expenses for travel, meals, and entertainment allowed by corporations to their employees—executives, in particular. However, these are fringes, or perks, that seem to outlast every president and IRS commissioner. They survive because many are necessary to the activities of the business world. Many are ordinary and necessary business expenses deductible on business tax returns. As the government becomes tougher on allowing such deductions, the companies become stricter in demanding receipts and reports to substantiate their reimbursements to employees on their corporate tax returns.

To add to the problem, inflation has progressively forced the companies to boost their allowances for such activities. Look at car allowances. While most companies allowed twelve cents a mile in 1972 and fifteen cents in 1977, many are now paying seventeen cents or more. Future boosts in gasoline prices will cause much larger increases in mileage allowances.

Other Perks

There are many other fringes for management employees. You, of course, realize that they are used to attract and keep executives. Obviously, the higher you are in the corporate structure, the more you can get not only in the number of benefits but also in the dollar value of the benefits. Such perks often include paid memberships in professional organizations, business associations, civic groups, and luncheon, social, or country clubs. Many executives are provided not only with a company car that can be used for personal activities but also with a reserved parking space in which to put the car. The company pays all maintenance and operating costs. Figure out for yourself how much you must receive *before* taxes to own and run an auto for one year.

Company-reimbursed travel and entertainment expenses can provide you with true entertainment while cutting your personal living costs as well. Some companies will provide periodic medical examinations. I predict that soon most companies will be paying for all medical and dental expenses not covered by insurance—premiums for the insurance are probably paid now by the company.

Some companies give counseling in career growth, personal finances, and legal and psychological matters. Many offer their executives free lunches in beautiful dining rooms, separate rest rooms with showers, and health or recreational facilities. If you are really up there, you may get kidnapping insurance, bodyguards, and security plans and devices for yourself, your property, and your family.

Let me remind you again to avoid discussion of fringes until after your salary has been set. Many of these fringes sound good, but it is your base salary and your bonuses, profit sharing, stock options, cost-reducing perks, and pension that count the most in the long run.

If you have qualms regarding your ability to negotiate, you should consider using some professional services, as described in the following chapter.

17

Professional Services for the Executive Job Searcher

There are many services available to help you in your search for a new position. Some are good and some are bad, and there must also be some that are both good and bad. Let us look at them to learn what types to use, how to use them, and what can be expected from them.

Employment Agencies

Employment agencies are the most numerous and widely known of these services. Despite their troubled history and the fact that only yesterday you may have read some adverse publicity about them, they do serve many people well, especially those seeking a job paying less than $20,000. This is simply because they look for volume business and are geared to handle many more people at, say, $10,000 than at $30,000. Also, companies looking for a clerk or secretary will obviously make those wants known to an employment agency rather than to an executive recruiter or other type of service.

Employment agencies are licensed by their respective states. Since they don't get paid unless their client/applicant is hired by a company, they tend to be order fillers rather than human beings earnestly trying to find the right slot for other human beings. All too often, the "counselors" you talk with at an employment agency are paid only the legal minimum wage *plus* a share of the fee when *they* successfully fill a job order. Therefore, they invest their time on the individuals they feel are most marketable.

Fees do vary but are mostly about 1 percent per $1,000, with set minimums and maximums. For instance, a $10,000 placement calls for a $1,000 fee. The fee on a $20,000 job can well be 20 percent or $4,000. The minimums usually average about 10 percent. I have seen maximums of 20 percent and even 25 percent.

Most agencies collect their fees from the employers. Although many agencies advertise that only employers pay their fees, some of these same agencies have asked applicants to sign forms actually listing possible situations under which the applicant will contractually owe the fee. Rule: Unless you are willing to pay the fee, do *not* sign any paper on which the fee schedule is printed. If the agency says it can't send you on an interview unless you sign, find another agency.

After all of this, why go to any agency? Because it can possibly find you an employer if your specialty and salary range fit its field. Some agencies are specialists in a type of work, such as warehouse personnel at all levels, stenographers, accountants, etc. Others are recommended for their work in a particular industry, such as retailing, finance, EDP, etc.

Obviously, you should try to see a few of the agencies specializing in your industry or your qualifications. Make a real effort to meet with the boss. If sold on you, he or she can make the staff work harder for you. Visit when you can get more attention. This means you should call only on a Tuesday, a Wednesday, or a Thursday afternoon.

Here is a place to use your resume. The agency probably can't work well without it. Make sure it does not make a broadcast mailing of it, even if the agency substitutes a code number for your name. Too many such mailings can kill your market. One of those mailings that I know of cost a man his job. The agency replaced the man's name with code number 344 and did not put in any company names. However, the resume was mailed to the best friend of his boss. The friend decided from the description of the duties outlined in the resume that applicant #344 had to be working directly for his buddy and therefore forwarded it. The boss recognized the man from the work history (functions) shown on the resume and immediately fired him by long-distance telephone.

Don't go to more agencies once you feel you have five that are truly capable and desirous of setting up good interviews for you. If an agency is knocking you or your ability to find an opening, it can't or won't help you. Retrieve your resume along with, if possible, any forms you filled out.

Being listed by more than five agencies can hurt your market, since the agencies don't just sit back waiting for job orders. They may try to sell you to their employer contacts over the phone or by mail. Repeated contacts by you or agencies to the same companies can be recognized and cost you a chance with those companies.

Executive-Placement Firms

Placement or executive-placement agencies can also be of help to you. These are firms that solicit job orders involving salaries usually in excess of $20,000. They don't often have openings for more than $40,000 and hardly ever for more than $50,000. I don't know of any that charge their fee to the applicant. They are similar to employment agencies in that they fill job orders and get paid only when their applicant gets the job. Do answer their ads.

Executive Searchers

Executive searchers (executive recruiters) also find people to fill job orders. Most of the better searchers do not work on speculation, as do the employment or placement agencies. Usually their search assignments involve managerial positions paying more than $40,000.

The searchers not working on speculation or contingency enter into a contract with the company desiring to find an executive. This contract covers their fees—probably 30 percent or more of the compensation to be paid—plus their out-of-pocket expenses. The fees are usually paid in three equal installments and are payable even if the search has not resulted in the acceptance of a new person by the time of the third installment.

A true searcher never collects a fee from the job hunter. His client is the company that retains him and hires the candidate.

Obviously, the executive recruiters are going to take a professional approach to filling their assignments. Typically, the candidates they present to their clients are employed, have a proved track record, and are very personable.

They find such people in many ways. Their personal contacts (some call them sources) are important. Executives who have become visible to the business world through their writings, work in a trade association or professional organization, or announcements in the newspapers or trade journals can expect a call or letter from a searcher if they fit the opening. The most important ingredient, however, is a record of successful and visible results on the job.

Most searchers will phone and some will write letters asking for help in finding a person qualified for a particular opening. If you receive such a letter or phone call, it may well be a feeler to find out whether you are interested in the position. If the searcher's initial contact is by letter, write asking for a copy of the job description if it was not sent with the letter and say you can be reached in your office or at home by phone. If the searcher initially calls you by phone either to ask whether you know somebody qualified or to directly ask about your interest, show your interest if you believe the opportunity justifies further exploration. Ask for additional information, such as the job description, annual reports, product literature, or whatever other data the search firm may have available. Remember, you are still going to be required to sell yourself as a person who can fill the requirements of the position.

Being employed, you may possibly worry lest your company find out about these conversations or correspondence. This is a needless concern. The recruiter is a professional and will provide confidentiality. You certainly know how to handle yourself to keep your own secret.

Searchers are not reluctant to present well-qualified but unemployed candidates to their clients. There is no such thing as "soiled goods" when it comes to consideration of able candidates. However, searchers who present more unemployed than employed candidates risk having their clients think of them as not doing much searching.

If you are, or were recently, earning more than $30,000, you should contact one hundred or more searchers by sales letter and resume. Make it a true sales letter—not a cover letter. See figures 29–33 for samples.

Fig. 29   A Letter to Executive Searchers

Jane Olson
910 North Gulch Blvd.
Spokane, Washington 99201
(509) 555-6080 home
(509) 555-0374 office

Date

Name, Title
Company
Street Address
City, State, Zip Code

Dear _____:

Food and beverage services, housekeeping, and facilities management
have been my strengths in the almost 20 years that I've been successfully comanaging a motel (actually two properties). I believe I can
bring a client organization added efficiencies as an administrator
of food and beverage or housekeeping functions.

As you can see from my resume, I have extensive, progressive, and
profitable experience in managing these areas. I am a motivated
woman who needs to give unstintingly of her time, effort, and
talents. I'd like to join a growing and appreciated organization
in the hotel, hospital, airline, club, or restaurant field.

May I have an interview regarding such a position with a client?
I look forward to a positive reply.

Sincerely,

Jane Olson

P.S. Earnings exceed $_____, plus the usual hotel/motel manage-
     ment perks.

Fig. 30   A Letter to Searchers from a Promotional Salesman

JOSEPH H. TELLER

2196 Birch Avenue * New Haven, Connecticut 06539 * (203) 555-6890 Home
(203) 555-6571 Office

Date

Name, Title
Company
Street Address
City, State, Zip Code

Dear _____:

Consumer and consumed goods require special sales and promotional
approaches. I've been beating budgets, setting new sales records,
and creating new products, services, and merchandising techniques
since 1959. Winning an award from a customer for developing a
promotional program is one of my greatest prides. The resulting
sale was $850,000.

Obviously, I'm trying to sell you on interviewing me for a sales-
management or sales-promotion-management position with a client.
Title isn't important—I'll happily accept a salesman position if
there is a chance to improve myself as I prove myself.

As shown on the resume enclosed, I am now an account executive
designing and selling merchandising programs, point-of-purchase
advertising displays, ad-specialty programs, incentive campaigns,
dealers' premiums, and various services or products that boost
sales.

Customers include rack jobbers, drug chains, department stores,
OEMs, supermarkets, advertising agencies, brewers, clothing manu-
facturers, franchisors, sporting-goods manufacturers, and several
GM divisions.

(This letter, if given to executive searchers, would be one page.)

To help improve sales, I have planned and managed award-winning trade show exhibits, customer golf tournaments, hospitality suites, cocktail parties, and sales-producing sales meetings for both customers and salespeople.

Have I earned that interview? Please call or write soon.

Sincerely,

Joseph H. Teller

P.S. Current earnings at $_____ plus expenses.

Fig. 31   A Marketing Executive's Approach to Executive Searchers

PETER F. PETRAK

190 Rosemary Lane * Atlanta, Georgia 30342 * (404) 555-1353 HOME
(404) 555-4011 OFFICE

Date

Name, Title
Company
Street Address
City, State, Zip Code

Dear _____:

Do you have a client who would be interested in hiring a responsible,
young, but widely experienced MBA for a MARKETING MANAGEMENT team?
I now have full profit responsibility for 60 retail centers. Their
marketing objectives are planned in my office and implemented through
area supervisors and retail managers under my direction. Therefore,
PRODUCT and SALES MANAGEMENT are also part of my responsibilities
and successful experiences.

Well rounded? I served on a four-man negotiating team for six
months to conclude the acquisition of a significant portion of a
major oil company ... I have served as Assistant Director of International Operations for a large chemical corporation ... as
Director of Retail Development for the same company, responsible for
complete selection and turnkey setup of 70 nationwide retail
operations ... as a member of the project team representing business
and commercial uses in designing a management information system ...
I was my company's representative in an extensive consulting analysis
of the distribution system using a top management consulting firm ...
I served on a three-man negotiating team working on a merger with a
large petroleum company.

Other important facts in my background are listed in the enclosed
resume. While going to college, I was employed as a research project
manager involved in behavioral research to determine public prefer-
ences for various media.

(This letter, if given to executive searchers, would be one page.)

I hope my variety of product, sales, and marketing experiences will induce you to contact me for an interview with one of your staff or a client. I look forward to hearing from you.

Sincerely,

Peter F. Petrak

P.S. Present earnings at $_____ level.

Fig. 32 A Letter to Recruiters

BERTRAM P. LANGLEY

9201 West 34th Street * St. Louis, Missouri 63151 * (314) 555-9211 HOME
                                                     (314) 555-1144 OFFICE

Date

Name, Title
Company
Street Address
City, State, Zip Code

Dear _____:

As engineering manager, I'm also a good salesman of engineered
products. Because of my ability to understand a customer's technical requirements and to mesh them into our product development,
I have built a reputation as a creative engineering manager who
helps build profitable products that fit the market's needs.

Last year I persuaded a customer to give us a $400,000 prepayment
on a computer system already two years behind delivery date. Of
course, I helped redesign the system while it was in production.

Electronic systems and controls for almost all types of needs are
my bread and butter. I have organized, staffed, and managed
engineering groups that developed new products, improved old products, analyzed competitive lines, and prepared long-range plans.

For my present employer, I formed an engineering group that is
responsible for manufacturing, engineering, and meeting customer
requirements of product lines whose volume increased fivefold.
More information is in the enclosed resume.

A BSEE, I also earned a BS in math. I'm writing to you, as I
believe I can fit a present or future search. I know I would
like to join a company as an engineering manager responsible
for product improvement, cost cutting, and/or customer contacts
on a technical basis.

Have I made real contact with you? An interview is requested to
really show you my potential with a client's firm.

Sincerely,

Bertram P. Langley

P.S. My compensation package is $_____.

Fig. 33 A Sales Letter to Executive Recruiters

EDWARD K. STRONG

6237 S. Kirwood * Memphis, Tennessee 38109 * (901) 555-8746 HOME
(901) 555-7776 OFFICE

Date

Name, Title
Company
Street Address
City, State, Zip Code

Dear _____:

If it's an office procedure, I've performed it ... and supervised
it. In fact, I've done it well enough to be promoted over the
years to Director of Employee Relations, Office Manager, and
Corporate Secretary of a construction company (not large). Degreed
in math, I began with this contractor as a bookkeeper and progressed
through other functions, such as cost accountant, payroll administrator, and even union negotiator.

This firm no longer offers me the challenge I need. That's why
I'm writing to you for an interview regarding a position with a
client.

You will find me to be well organized personally and an office
manager or administrator who organizes systems and people to get
the jobs done efficiently. As the enclosed resume shows, I'm a
good recruiter, trainer, supervisor, and developer of personnel.
I have developed centralized hiring and training systems for my
employer that are saving big dollars in investments and taxes and
slashing downtime on the various work sites.

How about that interview? Let me show you how my intelligence,
capabilities, and knowledge can produce for a client.

Sincerely,

Edward K. Strong

P.S. My compensation: $_____.

There are many, many lists of executive recruiters available. The problem with all lists is obsolescence. You can expect many to have developed some incorrect addresses or people since they were printed. My own list is updated after each use for a client. There are usually about 120 of what we consider to be the better firms on the list. We've never done a mailing without having to change from one to five individual names or firm addresses even if an update was made a few weeks or days earlier.

Your library can provide lists. Just ask the research librarian. If you are an AMA member, write to American Management Associations at 135 West 50th Street, New York, New York 10020, for their listing. You can get listings of the members of the Association of Executive Recruiting Consultants at 30 Rockefeller Plaza, New York, New York 10020, and the Association of Consulting Management Engineers located at 347 Madison Avenue, New York, New York 10017, has many firms doing executive searches. These are so indicated in their membership list.

There are some important differences between your sales letter to recruiters and a sales letter to prospective employers. Since you are not looking for a job with the recruiters, you will refer to your ability to fit a present or future search assignment. Send a resume to the searchers with your letter because some do not read letters that come in without resumes. These sales letters and resumes should show your home telephone number and your business number, especially if you can be dialed direct. If the recruiters are interested in you for a current opening when your letter comes in, you will probably be called at your office or at home if there is no alternative. If they feel you might fit a future assignment, they will probably classify your resume by industry and functional codes. It will then be filed for future retrieval.

Make sure your resume sent to search firms clearly identifies current and past employers. Resumes without this information are usually discarded because of the difficulty in ascertaining industry and/or product familiarity. Without company names, it becomes nearly impossible to track down an individual who has moved. The resume you send a search firm today may serve years hence as an introduction to a better job than the one you'll get now.

Your sales letter and/or resume should clearly outline your job titles and functions rather than give fuzzy, general career objectives, such as "A position in management in which I can utilize my experience and education." The letter (not the resume) to searchers should outline your current compensation package. This is contrary to what you would do in a general sales-letter mailing to industry.

You should also give search firms information as to the scope of your activities, such as the dollar volume for which you are responsible and the size of your staff. Play down the sales pitch. Play up the facts!

Make sure your presentation properly represents you as a qualified manager.

The searchers might not tell you the name of the company in initial interviews. At the same time, however, they will expect you to answer all their questions.

Be sure to answer the salary questions. By holding back too much, you may be dropped from consideration if there are equally good candidates with less reluctance. The clients are very definite about their compensation specifications and will demand hard data on any candidate before granting an interview or agreeing to pay any travel expenses.

If your compensation package is low because of a company or industry problem, explain the situation. There is nothing wrong in asking how much the company is planning to pay.

As I said before, in working with executive searchers who are actually commissioned by a company to fill executive-level positions, you are working with professionals. Hold your head high, be positive and cooperative. You will be one of their recommended candidates if you are qualified. The searchers are not going to do the actual hiring. They will provide their client with more than one applicant qualified to fill the post. They should be able to tell you many things about the job, the company, the people in it, and, most important, the hiring motivation. You must know the company's problem(s) to be solved— the mountains to climb—to come out on top in each interview.

Resume Writers

There are still other services available to the serious job searcher. Resume writers are located in the major cities. They will not only write your resume but also print it for you. You should at least initially compose your own resume. The first phase of your job-search campaign was learning the product—you. In recording your job functions, titles, and accomplishments, you provided yourself with data that should be distilled down to the better selling points to go into your resume as you embark on the second phase.

If you are not pleased with the resume as you wrote it, you can check it out with a knowledgeable executive, or you may prefer the help of resume writers. Be sure to see some resumes they have done so that you can be sure your resume won't look like all their others. After they have written it by using what you put in your original resume, you and only you should have the last word regarding anything in it. By all means, do not let them circularize it for you. Your mailing should be a sales letter. The resume is only a tool that will probably become necessary to use after initial contacts are made.

Consulting (?) Firms with Mailing Lists

Another service for the job hunter is available from firms that will take you on as a client, prepare various sales tools, and then send them to companies on their mailing lists. Their charge to you is minimal because they charge the company that hires you a fee of about 20 percent of your first year's salary. This would be a good deal for you if only they were more successful in placing their clients. Yes, many will refund your fee *if* they receive the larger fee.

Before signing up with one of those firms, it would be well to realize that it is to their benefit to limit your market to companies that will pay them a commission. Be sure to examine their credentials. These should include testimonials from individuals in your industry or in your line of work. Phone some of their clients to verify the work done for them and the results.

The firms may tell you their client list must be kept confidential, and therefore they cannot show you names. Not true. If they do a good job, many of their clients will be happy to act as references.

Be wary of any such firm that advertises it has job orders to fill. As with employment agencies, rarely does an applicant or a client get those great jobs.

Job Registers

Job registers and computerized matching services are also available to the job hunter. They claim to have listings of openings and for a small fee will match you with one or more of these opportunities. They make their money from the company if you are hired. They usually make mass mailings of coded (no names shown) resumes. This can overexpose you. It also limits your prospects to companies on their mailing list, as it presents you to these companies along with scores of other people. *Hardly a good sales approach for you.*

Want-Ad Clipping Services

Some firms will sell you a subscription to their want-ad clipping service. They will mail you reprints of ads from twenty-five to fifty newspapers once a week. This is a good source for you if they get the ads to you within a few weeks of publication. I personally know of such mailings that included ads a few months old. On ads I placed to hire a manager a few years ago, I received replies two and three months after the job had been filled. These late replies all mentioned they had seen my ad in the *recent* edition of a particular clipping service. Since the service never approached me for a fee, I cannot figure out why it asked its subscribers to mention its name—especially when the replies were so late.

Personal Marketing Consultants—Career Consultants

Next we come to the firms providing many services for the individual who wants to improve or change careers and find a new position. They call themselves executive consultants, personal marketing consultants, career counselors, executive marketers, etc. There are some very good firms in this field; but many are mediocre or average, and some are downright bad.

The good firms will help you set realistic career goals and then work with you to achieve at least the first goal. Some will follow up with you *after* you are in your new position.

Having been in this field for almost fifteen years, I am very biased in my thinking about these firms—both for and against them.

I believe in working with a psychologist to help the client set a series of attainable career goals. The psychologist and I will discuss strengths and weaknesses with each client individually and confidentially. We will counsel our clients on how to capitalize on their strengths and how to correct or at least modify the impact of their weaknesses. We place importance on their *true* motivations. What needs must be satisfied to make them happy with a job? This also tells us how much structure they need from a boss or a company. Do they belong in a large or a small organization? To sum it up: What would provide true career satisfaction for each individual?

Then the work begins! A firm like this will create complete marketing campaigns to fit the clients, their job functions, and their markets. Marketing tools, including resumes and sales letters, are prepared. I believe I should teach the clients how to think about a sales letter so that *they* can write a good one—subject to my editing. Like any true professional in this field, I will write their resume *after* they write one first. Of course, my versions are subject to their editing. Actually, nothing is used that both my clients and I do not agree on. Other sales tools are prepared and explained fully to them.

The consulting firm or consultant must wear many hats in doing a job for you. Your consultant should provide psychological support and *must* serve as your advertising manager and advertising writer, your marketing manager, your sales manager, and, finally, as your financial adviser in evaluating and possibly renegotiating your offers.

The marketing campaign is taught to the clients in a series of one-to-one meetings, as are interviewing and negotiating techniques. This is all personalized, since no two people interview alike. Personalities, strengths, weaknesses, and the type of jobs under consideration all affect how a person will interview and negotiate.

Our clients not only meet with us often but are also encouraged to phone us with questions as the marketing proceeds. We want to talk with them about each interview both before and after it takes place. We demand the right to evaluate each offer with the clients for their protection as well as ours. Their contracts provide further services from us *if* they accept positions that fit the career goals and psychological profiles originally established and we have evaluated these positions affirmatively.

Good personal marketing consultants will put their clients' needs first and foremost. This means they will do what they think is best for the client at all times. For example, if they feel a particular offer of a job is wrong for the client, they will not endorse it solely in hope the client will accept that job and thus lighten their work load. They will be very careful with any mailings. They will see to it that they are of top quality and go only to a list personally approved by the client.

How do you select a good personal marketing consultant or marketing consultant firm? Set up appointments with more than one. It is very possible you can be turned off by some. Continue till you find one who exhibits reasons for meriting your confidence. Ask to see proof of results and phone some of their ex-clients. *Get the background history of the people you would be working with. Insist on meeting the person who would be your consultant.* Determine that for the price you'll pay, you are going to have personalized attention—not meet as part of a class or group with your consultant. Get an idea as to how many such meetings you will have. Don't be sold by any reference to their corporate contacts. I personally know hundreds of senior-level executives, but they won't hire you just because you are my client. Why should your market be limited to a consulting firm's contacts?

The consulting firm you choose should be one in which you have confidence. This means confidence in everybody you meet with before you retain it. Any talk about the firm's having offices from coast to coast or in the area where you would like to move is just that—talk. The out-of-town offices are not going to be working with you or for you. They have their own clients with a demand on their time and loyalty. They are probably franchises financially interested only in their own operations.

Further, in checking the firms be sure to read the contract carefully. Be sure it spells out the procedures they sold to you. Is there a time limit on their services? Are there any extra costs now shown that were not mentioned before the contract was shown to you?

Perhaps you will want to check the firms out with your local Better Business Bureau and possibly with your state's attorney general's consumer fraud division. I owe it to my readers to remind them there are bad as well as good firms in this field. A good one will guide, coach, and market you into the right job and continue with you till that goal is reached. If you can use such help, find a good firm.

We often hear clients say they wish they had gone through our program five, ten, or fifteen years earlier. They say this because they have learned how certain behavior characteristics have impeded their advancement. Others, after they are in the new position, write such comments as "I can affirm unequivocally that signing up with . . . was the smartest investment I ever made." This letter came from the Vice-President–Finance of a $200-million New York Stock Exchange corporation.

This "investment" is tax deductible. Fees paid for this type of service plus your expenses in seeking a job are deductible as long as the job sought is not too dissimilar from your present or last job and you are not unemployed for an unusual length of time before starting this new job search. The deduction would still apply even if you later decided to remain with your present company. (We have also taught clients how to get promotions or transfers where they are.) However, the fees are not deductible if you are seeking your first job.

Corporate Outplacement Consultants

Terminated executives have yet another service available to them. This is a relatively new field called corporate outplacement. Because of economic shifts, high unemployment, and rising feelings of corporate responsibility, many companies provide outplacement service for people they fire. It is almost always accompanied by termination pay to bridge the financial gap until the new job is found.

Some personal marketing consultants described in this chapter also serve as corporate outplacement consultants. The only differences are that the company discharging the client pays the fee, and the fee is usually higher than the individual would pay for the same service. Note that the individual was referred to as the client even though the company paid the fee. The individual must be considered the client, since the consultant is working with him or her constantly and should keep that person's particular needs in mind at all times. The consultant can do this without hurting any relationship with the company.

If you are discharged, do talk to the company regarding outplacement. The company may send you to one or two consultants with whom it has dealt before. You should also see some firms on your own. Use the same processes as those described for choosing a personal marketing consultant. It is your life and your future at stake. Although it is the company's money, the company is almost always willing to let you choose your consulting firm.

As proof that some companies can have a real feeling for people they discharge, I want to tell you about two incidents. Bill S. was sent to an outplacement consultant. After almost four months of utter frustration, he came to us and signed up as a client at his own expense. One month later he wrote to his company to tell it how bad its choice had been, praised our work, and asked the company to repay him the fee he had paid us. The company, one of the largest in the world, repaid him. It also sent us another outplacement who had refused to go to the first consultant. A major insurance company paid us to take over the failures of yet another consultant. These cases represent double payments by the companies.

A company sent us an executive they had fired two years prior. In that period he had been unable to find a new position, and they felt a responsibility for him.

Again I remind you that in corporate outplacement, there are also varying degrees of skill and professionalism. Find the consulting organization in which you have confidence. This confidence was gained by the methods described above for selecting a personal marketing consultant. Never turn down good outplacement service, as it will be of real help to you without any investment of money on your part.

Use of professional services also provides something no book, including this one, can give—the answer to each of the many problems and questions that come up again and again in your job-search campaign. In working with hundreds of clients for all these years, I must have answered tens of thousands of questions. One client I will never forget had twelve meetings with me and phoned me seventy-eight times. For each meeting and each phone call, she had a list of questions prepared in advance. The last meeting and the last three phone calls took place after she had started her new job. In a few months I'm sure I answered more than three hundred questions for her.

I am sure that within the next month I will be asked many questions never asked of me before. I am afraid you won't find the answers to those questions in this or any other book. Even if all the questions could be covered in one book, you'd be bored reading it, since a great majority of them would not cover your particular needs.

Also, I too would be bored if all the questions, problems, and needs of all my clients were identical. I would not have the day-to-day challenges of overcoming various problems and obstacles to satisfy the needs of different clients.

I am also personally stimulated when I teach my clients on a very personalized basis how to progress beyond the new job we helped them find. There is useful information for you in chapter 18 on how to advance your career.

18

On the New Job

The day you start in your new position is the day you start looking and preparing for your next one! No, I'm not preaching disloyalty. I am preaching loyalty to what should be number one—yourself. Your next position will probably be with your new firm but with higher rank and salary.

The first few months on any job is a combination of a honeymoon and a probationary period. It is a honeymoon because you were hired with great expectations. Your new boss wants you to succeed. After all, he or she hired you, and your success makes him or her look good while at the same time lowering the work load.

On the other hand, you are on probation because the newcomer is always watched a bit more closely. However, the honeymoon syndrome will allow you to get away with some errors that would provoke real censure if committed by an employee of long standing.

Look Before You Leap

Start off by being a good listener. Find out not only how but why things are done the way they are, no matter how different they may be from methods you know to be tried and true. Learn and look before you suggest any important changes.

Start a Hero File

To pave the way for promotions and raises—or for a job with yet another company—there are several actions you should initiate as you begin with your new employer. Do you remember the interview kit described earlier in this book? It was probably difficult to create it because you had not realized any need for it before you started your hunt for this position. *Now* is the time to start gathering materials together, either as an interview kit for a later job-search campaign or as a "hero file" to further your progress with the new company.

An important part of your hero file can be a diary of your accomplishments, thoughts, and actions. Record such items at least once a week.

Be sure your file contains copies of memos or letters that reflect well on your abilities. Include proofs of your measurable accomplishments. These proofs can be carbon copies or photocopies of sales you have made, letters or memos from customers or bosses—anything that shows you have been doing a good job.

For example, I have received hundreds of thank-you letters from my clients telling me of the successful results of the job-search campaigns I created, managed, and controlled for them. While the originals are in my office, as they are actually company property, I have photocopies of most of them in my home in case I need them to find a job for myself. I am hoping that in reading this, *you* will practice what *I* preach and practice for myself.

Obviously, this hero file will be very helpful if you ever need it to write another resume, prepare for more interviews, or write a new sales letter.

When and How to Ask the Bosses to Critique You

The hero file will also be very helpful on the new job. You should review your progress with your new superior at proper times. You may be up for a performance and/or salary review after six or twelve months on the job. Don't wait that long to obtain *constructive* criticism from the person who has the most control over your future in the company. Read and reread your hero file after you have been there two or three months. Then someday when your boss is in a good mood, preferably after you have been paid a compliment, ask for a few minutes to discuss how you are doing. Say that you naturally would like to hear what you are doing right. But even more important, you want to know the areas in which you can improve. You want to make changes that will make you of more value to your superiors, the company, and yourself. (Note the order of importance.)

This approach may enable you to learn something that will be of benefit to your future. Because your superior is in a good mood when you two talk, he or she may possibly say nice things that force him or her to do better for you when the six- or twelve-month review comes up.

Perhaps you should talk again about a month prior to the time scheduled for the performance/salary review. Make sure of your timing. The boss should be in a good mood. Now you can afford to be a bit more casual. Ask if the improvements in you that were fostered by the previous meeting were noticed. Your boss will probably realize you are doing this because of the review coming up. This lets the powers-that-be know that you are trying (and hopefully succeeding) and are truly interested in working to better your position with the company.

In this second meeting or at the review itself, you should ask questions regarding your future with the company.

Be a Politician

The day you start this new job is also the day you become more political. Since this is not intended to be a book on office politics, it will confine itself to saying you should always try to retain your objectivity. Don't be subjective. Try always to see the *whole* picture. Work on improving your communication skills. Realize good politics are positive interpersonal relationships. Good politicians will keep their aim on their long-range objectives. This means they will do what they feel is best for their future even though they may not completely agree it is the right thing for now. Good politicians go out of their way to please their superiors rather than antagonize them with forceful disagreements. They will suggest other approaches to handle a matter but will wholeheartedly follow whatever decision the boss makes in the end.

Act and Talk like the Bosses

As a politician you will also watch the actions and even the mannerisms of the key people in the company. This means you must first
identify who the key people really are. Many clients have told me
their company was run by one person. Further questioning usually
brought out the fact that this one person listened to, and worked
closely with, one or two other corporate officers. Watch these top
people. Study their mannerisms. Listen to how they talk. Learn their
jargon. Every industry and every company has its own vocabulary.
Start talking the new language as soon as possible. In other words,
now that you have identified the true key people in the organization,
you are going to identify *with* them. They cannot help but like the
person who acts, talks, and thinks their way. Often they do not realize
consciously just why they like one person over others.

Become Visible in Your Industry

The first few months on the job are critical because you are laying the
groundwork for your future with the company. Do not let anything
interfere with your work activities during that time. Later, when you
have a handle on the job, start to broaden your scope. Strive for
visibility. Join trade or professional organizations. Talk to people both
inside and outside your industry. Attend trade shows. Read everything you can about your industry and your own field within the
industry. Write articles for trade journals or other business publications. Make speeches. Teach. Compete for industry awards. Volunteer to lead. Do everything time and ability permit to attain that
visibility. Your bosses will be proud of you, and outsiders will learn
about you. Someday you may unexpectedly hear from an executive
searcher about a better job. Perhaps competitors or members of your
association may "knock on your door" to discuss a position with
them.

Keep Current Technically

While striving for visibility, you should also be tuned in to changes in
your field. This will keep you current and efficient in your daily work.

In fact, it will make you appear innovative and possibly creative to your superiors.

Always Know Your Job Market

You should also keep abreast of the job market as it pertains to your future. Read the want ads. You might answer a few, if only to learn your present value in the marketplace. Use a friend's name with permission or a fake name if you have fears of getting caught.

The purpose of this book is to show you how to find a better job. This chapter goes even one more step and perhaps will lead you from that better job into another or *best* job. How can anyone define the best job? It really is the *right* job. It is the position in which you feel fulfilled. You have a sense of belonging, accomplishing, and doing good for others as well as yourself. It is the job you can't wait to get to each morning.

This Book Will Help You Get There!

Now you know how to find not only the better job but also the best job. Go to work on it immediately. Use the marketing tools provided, such as the Interview and Lead Report Forms. Feel free to reproduce as many of them as you need. Reread the pertinent chapters as you reach each phase in your job-search campaign. Think in positives only. Almost everybody has high and low spots when job hunting. Expect them and use them as the basis for your positive approaches.

Good luck! Good hunting!